THE BEAST OF THE EAST

ALVIN M. SHIFFLETT

TimeLee BOOKS™

STARBURST PUBLISHERS™

P.O. Box 4123, Lancaster, Pennsylvania 17604

To schedule Author appearances write:
Author Appearances, Starburst Promotions, P.O. Box 4123,
Lancaster, PA 17604 or call (717)-293-0939.

Credits:

Cover art by Dave Ivey

Unless otherwise noted, all Scripture quotations are from the NIV.

We, The Publisher and Author, declare that to the best of our knowledge
all material (quoted or not) contained herein is accurate; and we shall
not be held liable for the same.

First Printing, May 1992

ISBN: 0-914984-41-1
Library of Congress Catalog Number 91-67060

Printed in the United States of America

This book is dedicated
to
Dick and *Marjorie Sechrist*,
two saints who have made this
world better until He comes.

In heaven,
to be even the least is a great thing,
where all will be great;
for all shall be called the children of God.
Thomas á Kempis

Contents

Contents—cont'd.

Prologue

On January 16, 1991 Coalition Forces under the Codename of Desert Storm, unleashed upon Iraq the greatest air assault in the history of warfare. In the first 30 days of the war over 50,000 sorties were flown. The first 24 hours of the war cost the U.S. over 300 million dollars. According to an article published in the *Myrtle Beach Sun News*, daily troop cost for the U.S. alone was over $74 million dollars (this estimate based on 452,000 U.S. troops including the reserves).

This war was text book high-tech. Smart bombs, such as the Tomahawk cruise missile, and the Patriot (anti-missile missile) each cost approximately $1.3 million. A hundred Tomahawk cruise missiles were fired in the first 24 hours of Desert Storm! A smart bomb like the Tomahawk can travel 500 miles and with pinpoint accuracy go through the upright beams of a goalpost. Military personnel tell me that a smart bomb could be fired from the Norfolk, Virginia, naval base and take out a Mister Donut shop in Myrtle Beach, South Carolina, if that were the target!

Prior to the war, Saddam Hussein, presidential monarch of Iraq, spent millions of dollars to build massive underground bunkers. Many of these bunkers were used in the long and costly eight year war with Iran. It was reported in the February 4, 1991 Issue of *Newsweek* that Saddam's personal bunker was a "lavishly decorated 12-room complex built in 1981 at a cost of $65 million dollars . . . the main entrance is a three-ton steel door; the impenetrable walls are lead-lined concrete, six feet thick. In a situation room (his war room), Saddam had available 24 TV screens, and he addressed his people from an adjacent broadcast studio. Interior designers from Munich furnished the family quarters with crystal chandeliers, plush carpets, a sauna, and a personal bedroom with a four poster bed covered with a red silk canopy. It was built to withstand atomic blasts, and even the toilets were tested for radiation! According to one German report, 25 people could live for a year in this underground fortified paradise."[1] No wonder Saddam thought of himself as a modern day King Nebuchadnezzar.

The elite Republican Guard, Iraq's crack combat-hardened troops, were also reported hunkered down in massive cavernous underground bunkers. Prior to the war, the Iraqi soldiers planted a million land mines in anticipation of the ground assault by Coalition forces. Desert Storm was no mini-war police action.

The Gulf War made it apparent to any biblical student that the white horse of Revelation Six had bolted from the gate and was racing across the sands of this ancient cradle of civilization. John, the writer of Revelation says:

> *I looked, and there before me was a white horse! Its rider held a bow, and he was given a crown, and he rode out as a conqueror bent on conquest.*
>
> Revelation 6:2

This first horse of the apocalypse has always been known as the war horse. It is not the same as the white horse of Chapter 19 of Revelation (see Report Seven), as the rider of that horse is called *The King of Kings and Lord of Lords* (See Revelation 19:16). This horse, of Revelation 6, represents war—the kind of war that unleashed hell's fury upon a nation for 30 days, and then ground out an unprecedented 100-hour ground assault.

PROLOGUE

I believe Desert Storm is the prelude to Armageddon. And that is why I have written this book. There are things yet to happen. Things that CNN and other national affiliates will not tell you. The fact is, they won't tell you because they don't believe these things will happen. But prior to the Gulf War, who would have believed the low casualties, and almost cataclysmic lightning-like ending? Alleged experts were all predicting just the opposite.

I'm not a late-date doomsday proponent. I'm not Nostradamus (who incidentally predicted the Lord would return in 1991), or any free-lance prophetic huckster seeking gain by sensationalizing apocalyptic notions. I'm just one of many of God's reporters down here in enemy territory—like Peter Arnett in Baghdad, who had the script prepared and handed to him. This script, however, unlike Peter's, can be trusted—it is the Bible.

I think many of us, for whatever reason, became irresponsible reporters. We got involved in a late-date theological system that made us real comfortable. We sort of hunkered down in our theological bunkers like the elite Iraqi Republican Guard, hoping that the rapture would take us out of this mess. We've made the rapture our anti-tribulatory patriot missile, and have said, "We'll be out of here when the Scuds start to fall!" We've relied entirely upon a high-tech air campaign: "I'll fly away," and ignored the words of our Commander-in-Chief:

In this world you will have trouble . . .
John 16:33

Anticipated casualties? Yes, for those who refuse to accept the total campaign plan. Disappointments? Yes, for those who persist on hunkering down with false theological theories. So my purpose in writing is twofold: (1) To eliminate the casualties, for He desires that all might be saved; and (2) To strengthen the faith of the faithful, in case of a long and arduous campaign, so that no one will be disappointed. For He promised:

And surely I am with you always, to the very end of the age.

Matthew 28:20

Report 1

THE FALL OF IRAQ

DESERT Storm was barely two weeks old when Saddam Hussein blatantly broke the Geneva Treaty with regards to treatment of prisoners of war. He paraded them on television and threatened that unless the bombings stopped, he would use the prisoners as human shields. Americans and the world were shocked and outraged. President Bush said that Saddam would be held personally responsible for ignoring the Geneva Treaty guidelines for treatment of POW's.

As one Marine put it, "The war, as it turned out, was a blitzkrieg, a mismatch—Rhode Island taking on the United States." It was a defeat of almost biblical proportions. Saddam Hussein's predicted "Mother of all Battles," quickly became the "Father of all Defeats." The low rate of American casualties in the war was, as General Schwarzkopf said, "almost miraculous." The British Commander, Peter de la Billiere, in retrospect exuded: "We are today, at the end of perhaps one of the greatest victories we have ever experienced. We needn't be shy about it. A great victory." President Bush, riding the crest of enormous popularity (91% in favor of the way he handled himself as Commander-in-Chief) said in reference to World War II, "There was a definitive end to that conflict, but in the Persian Gulf War, we have Saddam still there, the man that wreaked this havoc upon his neighbors . . . "

The aftermath of all this was civil war. In order to crack down on internal unrest, Saddam sacked his Interior Minister and replaced him with Ali Hassan Majid, a cousin accused of using chemical weapons on the Kurds. Majid is the second Saddam cousin named to the Cabinet in six months, and is the one responsible for many atrocities—torture, rape, illegal arrests, etc. An International Relations professor at Boston University said: "It's obvious that Saddam is trying to quell the uprising at any costs." The Iranian (ancient Persia) President Rafsanjani, denounced Saddam at Friday prayers in Tehran and called for him to "submit to the will of the people and step down." But as of this writing, Saddam, who calls himself the "Sword of the Arabs," and likes to be compared to Nebuchadnezzar, appears to have survived the Gulf defeat and civil unrest.

The Middle East, it seems, continues in apocalyptic turmoil. The dream for peace between the Arab and Jew appears to be just that—a dream. In order to understand this turmoil, and its apocalyptic nature, we need to take a scan-aramic look at the Genesis of this area to discover the birth of these present day problems.

The Cradle Of Civilization

The beginning of humankind started in this area of Mesopotamia (land between the rivers) referred to as the Fertile Crescent. It was in this area of the Tigris/Euphrates Rivers that God planted (made) a garden. In this all-sufficient garden God placed Adam and Eve, the father and mother of civilization.

The location of Eden, has been much in̩
ancient and modern times. The data given in ᴄ
sufficient to help us fix an exact location. Mainl̦y
two of the rivers mentioned in Genesis no longer exist. ᴧe
Genesis account reads:

> *A river watering the garden flowed from Eden; and from there it was separated into four headwaters. The name of the first is the Pishon; it winds through the entire land of Havilah, where there is gold . . . The name of the second river is the Gihon; it winds through the entire land of Cush. The name of the third river is the Tigris; it runs along the east side of Asshur. And the fourth river is the Euphrates.*
> Genesis 2:10-14

Due to the Gulf War, just about everyone in the world now knows where the Tigris and Euphrates Rivers are located. Newspapers and magazines proliferated maps of the Middle East, in particular of Iraq. We've seen bridges being blown up on the Tigris and Euphrates Rivers. In the initial stages of the war an activist peace group was encamped on an island in the Euphrates River. Many modern day scholars suggest that the district at the head of the Persian Gulf was the likely location of Eden. It was believed that silt carried by the rivers added over a hundred miles to the head of the Persian Gulf since 3000 B.C. But more recent geological examinations suggest it may not have changed much from ancient times. A short distance from the ancient site of Babylon, which is approximately 50 miles south of Baghdad, the Tigris and Euphrates Rivers flow so close together that canals connect them. It is in this area that Delitzsch and others feel is the proper location of Eden.[2]

The Ancient City Of Babylon

The historical remains of the ancient city of Babylon lies just fifty miles south of Baghdad, capital of Iraq, along the river Euphrates. The influential city was lined with palm trees and possessed a permanent water supply which guaranteed fertility in the area. It was within easy reach of the Persian Gulf, and situated on an important caravan trade route.

The date of Babylon's founding is disputed, but it probably reached its zenith of power and influence during the reign of King Nebuchadnezzar II (605-562 B.C.). Under Nebuchadnezzar's rule, Babylon, noted for its fabled hanging gardens, was probably the largest and most elaborate city in the ancient world. In 1978, Saddam Hussein began rebuilding the ancient city of Babylon. Until that time, all that remained of the former glory was a series of mounds some five miles in extent, lying mostly on the left bank of the Euphrates River. Originally, the city occupied an area of about 200 square miles, and was built on both sides of the Euphrates.

The massive Ishtar Gate guarded the northern entrance of the city. This gate was decorated with enameled brick reliefs of bulls and dragons, while the walls of the avenue approaching it depicted a possession of snarling lions. Southwest of the Ishtar Gate was the huge *ziggurat* of Babylon, which was closely linked with the temple of Marduk. The ground plan of the ziggurat was approximately 300 feet square. The structure, as it stood in the sixth century B.C., exceeded 300 feet in height. Many think this great ziggurat was the ancient Tower of Babel (Genesis 11:1-9). During the recent Gulf War, Saddam ordered MIG-29 Fulcrum fighters parked next to the ancient ziggurat for protection. He knew the Coalition Forces would not bomb there for fear of destroying a historical site. Or, perhaps he hoped they would bomb the site giving him a propaganda coup. Then he would have shown the world how the uncultured "infidels" destroy historical sites!

The old Babylonian Empire consisted of all present day Iraq and Kuwait, portions of Syria and Turkey, and included the all important headwaters of the Tigris and Euphrates Rivers. In our modern day world, the major portion of territory of ancient Babylon is probably best represented by Iraq. Indeed, Saddam Hussein thinks of himself as becoming the leader of the Muslim world. The theme of the 1987 Babylonian Festival held on the historical site was: "From Nebuchadnezzar to Saddam Hussein, Babylon Undergoes A Renaissance."[3]

Obviously, the recent war has caused a major setback in Saddam's plans. Had he been able to hold on to oil-rich Kuwait, he would have been one of the most powerful leaders since Alexander the Great. It will be interesting to watch and see if Saddam can rise again like a Phoenix from the ashes of defeat and pursue his dream. A dream of uniting the Arab world under his leadership, and re-establishing the Babylonian Empire. If this ever happens it will be bad news for Israel! Saddam knows that Nebuchadnezzar was the only Arab ruler ever to lead Arab armies against the Israelites and defeat them. In the Nebuchadnezzar Museum of partially rebuilt Babylon, Saddam has carefully chosen colorful murals depicting the life of the ancient emperor. One mural shows Nebuchadnezzar in battle against a city. It is obvious that the city in the mural is in a mountainous region surrounded by a prominent valley— Jerusalem. Saddam Hussein wants to parallel the life of Nebuchadnezzar by leading his army against the Jews of Jerusalem![4]

The Babylonian Empire was used by God to carry Israel into seventy years of captivity. One of those deported from Israel to Babylon was the prophet Daniel. Daniel did his reporting from the capital (Babylon), just as Peter Arnett did his censored reporting from Iraq's present capital, Baghdad.

Both reporters, Daniel and Peter Arnett, apparently gained favor with the ruling powers. The difference being, Daniel, although a prisoner of Babylon, was God's influential man in advising Kings Nebuchadnezzar, Belshazzar, and Darius the Mede. Whereas, Peter Arnett, who was in Baghdad for CNN, had no influence over Saddam Hussein. The opposite may have been the case as Saddam sought to use Arnett and CNN to influence the world and divide the Coalition Forces arrayed against him. Fortunately, it failed.

Had Saddam taken his case into diplomatic circles he would have had a strong argument for making Kuwait his 19th Province. (We Americans tend to perceive borders drawn since World War I as permanent.) From the Iraqi perspective, however, and the ancient Babylonian Empire, these borders are fairly recent and drawn by Colonial powers. Indeed, during the last 2,000 years Mesopotamia has spent 95% of its history incorporated into a bigger territory than present day Iraq. Over 50% of that time Mesopotamia controlled most or all of the Tigris/Euphrates headwater. For at least 80% of its history it controlled Kuwait and the mouth of the two rivers.[5]

Large areas shared sovereignty with Iraq in times past. Egypt, Libya, the Saudi Arabian peninsula, parts of Iran, and the Soviet Union, as well as Turkey shared sovereignty with Iraq for 500 years. Kuwait, parts of Syria, Turkey, and Iran shared sovereignty with Iraq for over 1,000 years. These are long times compared with the short history of the U.S. of 200 years. It also reveals the explosiveness of the area.[6]

The World's Most Dangerous Man?

The June 4, 1990 issue of *U.S. News & World Report* carried a picture of Saddam on the cover with the caption: "The Most Dangerous Man in the World." During the last decade he has been the world's single biggest buyer on the international market of chemical, biological, and nuclear weaponry. It has been estimated that he spent over $50 billion to build his army, which was literally destroyed within a month. Saddam knew exactly what he was about. He was not a madman, but had visions of grandeur—like Nebuchadnezzar, or Alexander the Great. Some even called him the Arab Hitler! It is well known by now that he had three ambitious goals:

(1) Territory

(2) Economic Power

(3) The total elimination of the nation of Israel

It is well documented that he said: "I swear by God, we will let our fire scorch half of Israel if it tries to wage anything against us." Apparently he never forgot that in 1981 the Israelis with a bold pre-emptive strike knocked out his nuclear bomb factory, which they reckoned was making bombs to use against them.

Saddam, the son of a peasant, is said to have committed his first murder at 14. At 20, he joined the underground Baath Party and reportedly tried to assassinate the ruler of Iraq. Failing, he fled to Syria. He rose to power in 1978 when a bloody coup took control of the Iraqi government. Since then he has been ruthless in his ways. Reports say Saddam once shot one of his own cabinet members at point blank range when he disagreed with him during a cabinet meeting. What ever happened to Robert's Rules of Order? He is said to have executed 120 of his officers who disagreed with his August 2 invasion and subsequent takeover of Kuwait. He had himself designated President of Iraq for life, and feels ordained by Allah to lead the Arab world to glory.

Saddam was, and still is powerful. Before the war he had the world's fourth largest army—a million man army. He

17

possessed an arsenal (many more than apparently estimated), of now famous long range Scud Missiles (obtained from the Soviet Union). He had a powerful air force and over 5,000 tanks. Desert Storm will be remembered as the final perfection of the blitzkrieg. Schwarzkopf's model—Montgomery versus Rommel at El Alamein—was fought on a far smaller scale. It pitted 1,200 Allied tanks versus 520 from the Afrika Korps. The Coalition Forces sent 3,500 tanks up against the surviving elements of the Republican Guard—probably about 2,000 tanks.[7]

Saddam is also well known for his chemical weapons, which he freely used during the Iranian War. He forced a cease fire by firing missiles on population centers in Iran and by using poisonous gas on Iranians and resistive Kurds. It is now known that he wiped out entire towns of Kurds.

Since his invasion of Kuwait he not only gained what he called his 19th Province, but an additional 275 tanks, 260 armored cars, 40 helicopters, 34 Skyhawks and 32 Mirages, 8 ships, and a vast arsenal of missiles. Plus he raided the wealthy Kuwaiti treasury of $4-5 billion in gold and currencies, which he desperately needed due to the Iranian War. Had Saddam been allowed to keep his new 19th Province, and rich Kuwaiti oil fields, he would have controlled 20% of the world's oil supplies.[8] Fortunately for the oil addicted western world, the new Babylonian Empire has been put on hold.

Regardless of what we say about Saddam Hussein, he is a survivor. His highly touted army has been decimated. His air force rendered totally ineffective, and for some strange reason 137 fighter jets were flown and parked in Iran. Civil war followed the Gulf War, but now Saddam has apparently regained the upper hand. But he faces enormous problems. Iraq now has a foreign debt of over $75 billion due to the costly eight year Iranian War. Plus their debt to the people and government of Kuwait could range upwards to $100 billion. Saddam is having a tough time convincing his people that they won a great victory over the western infidels on Iraqi sand. In the long run, Saddam Hussein may not survive, but Iraq will. I believe the Word of God confirms this, as Syria, Iraq, and Iran will all be major players in the final run toward Armageddon. But more on this later.

Did Jeremiah See Desert Storm?

Jeremiah 50 and 51 depicts the certain and sure fall of Babylon into the hands of the Assyrians. Babylon gave way to the Medo-Persian Empire under Cyrus in 537 B.C. This conqueror did not pillage Babylon, but acted respectfully toward the Shrines and deities of the land. Enslaved populations were liberated, including many Hebrews, and Cyrus set about building up the Persian Empire. Later, when the Persian Empire fell to Alexander the Great in 330 B.C., Babylon was destroyed fulfilling the prophecies of Jeremiah . . . to a point. After this, Babylon steadily declined in importance, except as a historical site for archaeologists. The present Baghdad to Bassorah railway passes within a few yards of the mound which was once the most splendid city of the ancient world.

I fully believe that Jeremiah 50 and 51 can also be applied to modern day Iraq. The prophecy is a case of being fulfilled once in history, and again eschatologically with Desert Storm. Saddam Hussein, at tremendous loss, was forcibly ejected from Kuwait. He should not have been surprised, as what happened to Iraq was forseen centuries ago by the prophet Jeremiah. Saddam should have read the Bible instead of the Koran. Listen to these words and see if you agree:

19

THE BEAST OF THE EAST

Prophetic Utterance:

> *The Lord has opened his arsenal and brought out the weapons of his wrath.*
> Jeremiah 50:25

Modern Application:

Missiles, bombs, and other high-tech weapons were used.

Prophetic Utterance:

> *Come against her from afar. Break open her granaries; pile her up like heaps of grain. Completely destroy her . . .*
> Jeremiah 50:26

Modern Application:

Depicted by U.S. led Coalition Forces.

Prophetic Utterance:

> *Look! An army is coming from the north; a great nation and many kings are being stirred up from the ends of the earth . . . they sound like the roaring sea . . .*
> Jeremiah 50:41-42

Modern Application:

Air strikes from Turkey and U.S. led Coalition Forces.

Prophetic Utterance:

> *See, I will stir up the spirit of a destroyer against Babylon . . . I will send foreigners to Babylon to . . . devastate her land.*
> Jeremiah 51:1-2

Modern Application:

Was this a prediction of President George Bush, who appeared unmoveable during the war, as if he had a "spirit of a destroyer?" The foreigners might be what Saddam referred to as western "infidels."

Prophetic Utterance:

Flee from Babylon! Run for your lives!
Jeremiah 51:6

Modern Application:

Refugees fled to Jordan during the war.

Prophetic Utterance:

Babylon's warriors have stopped fighting; they remain in their strongholds . . .
Jeremiah 51:30

Modern Application:

The Iraqi soldiers remained in fortified bunkers, and surrendered by the thousands when the ground assault started.

Prophetic Utterance:

The sea will rise over Babylon; its roaring waves will cover her. Her towns will be desolate . . . waves of enemies will rage like great waters; the roar of their voices will resound. A destroyer will come against Babylon.
Jeremiah 51: 42, 55-56

Modern Application:

The world watched by television as B-52's and wave after wave of aircraft struck at Baghdad and other strategic sites in Iraq.

THE BEAST OF THE EAST

The destruction that Desert Storm rained upon Iraq never happened with the initial fall of Babylon to Cyrus. Cyrus diverted the River Euphrates and walked in and took over the city—lock, stock, and barrel. The pictures on television of the total devastation of Iraq, due to the air war, seem more apropos to Jeremiah's words than at any other time in history. Desert Storm may indeed be the long awaited fulfillment of the ancient prophet's warnings.

Report 2

ISRAEL

THE Twentieth Century has witnessed one of the most dramatic events in world history—a restoration of an ancient people to their land. In 1948 Israel was again recognized as a nation among the United Nations. The story of Israel's resurrection goes back thousands of years to Ur of the Chaldees in Mesopotamia (modern-day Iraq).

Abram was called by God in Genesis Chapter 12:

Leave your country, your people and your father's household and go to the land I will show you.
                                               Genesis 12:1

Through Abram, who later would be renamed Abraham (Father of Nations), God made some magnificient promises— which He always keeps, as God cannot lie and is immutable (non-changing). He promised Abraham that he would: (1) Make him a great man. [His name is revered by Jew, Christian, and Muslim.] (2) Make his posterity great. [He is the father of Jews and Arabs]. (3) Through him all the families of the earth would be blessed. God promised that those who befriended and blessed Abraham [and his posterity] would be blessed, and those who oppressed or opposed Abraham and his posterity would be cursed (Genesis 12:3). History has witnessed these judgements or curses upon the enemies of Israel over the centuries: Egypt, Assyria, Babylon, Rome, and in modern times Spain, Germany, Russia, and today—Iraq. There are more judgements to come![9]

The Gift Of Land

It is interesting to note the territory promised to Abraham, which by the way, has never been changed. In Genesis 15, the Bible gives a clear description of the boundary lines of Israel:

> *On that day the Lord made a covenant with Abram and said, "To your descendants I give this land, from the river of Egypt to the great river, the Euphrates—the land of the Kenites, Kenizzites, Kadmonites, Hittites, Perizzites, Rephaites, Amorites, Canaanites, Girgashites and Jebusites."*
>
> Genesis 15:18-21

Many people, ignorant of God's covenants today, do not realize the extent of this covenant. God promised to Abraham a vast territory that still is not controlled by Israel. The land promised was Palestine, stretching from the Sinai desert north and east to the Euphrates River, which as everyone knows today would include present day Israel, Jordan, Lebanon, parts of Syria, Iraq (to the Euphrates), and some of Saudi Arabia. Think of that! This promise was made by God as an "everlasting covenant." It was **not** based on any specific conditions of obedience, or anything that Israel might do to merit it. There is considerable disagreement as to whether or not Israel has ever possessed all the land God promised to them. Regarding the territory God promised to Abraham, Leupold says: "Twice during Israel's history this extent of territory was realized, during the reign of Solomon (I Kings 8:65), as well as in the days of Jereboam II of Israel (II Kings 14:25) . . . such a measure of territory definitely put Israel into the category of the first-class nations of the world, even though but temporarily."[10]

In I Kings 4:20-21 we have an even stronger statement apropos the fulfillment of this covenant:

The people of Judah and Israel were as numerous as the sand on the seashore; they ate, they drank and they were happy. And Solomon ruled over all the kingdoms from the River (Euphrates River) to the land of the Philistines, as far as the border of Egypt. These countries brought tribute and were Solomon's subjects all his life.

So God did keep His word and gave all the land He had promised to Abraham and his seed. The fulfillment of this promise is also recorded in Joshua 21:43-45:

*So the Lord gave Israel **all** the land he had sworn to give their forefathers, and they took possession of it and settled there.*

Bad Blood

Actually Israel's present day problems stem from a foolish decision Abraham made with Sarah (earlier called Sarai) his wife. God had made an everlasting covenant with Abraham, and promised that his posterity would inherit the land and the subsequent blessings of the covenant. However, there was one major problem. Sarah was barren. Abraham became impatient for a son and Sarah sensing this, suggested they help God fulfill His promise. So she said to Abraham:

The Lord has kept me from having children. Go, sleep with my maidservant; perhaps I can build a family through her.

Genesis 16:2

Abraham agreed to this arrangement before Sarah changed her mind, and upon sleeping with Hagar (the maidservant) she conceived. But a desert storm was brewing. Sarah became jealous. Each day the ever increasing evidence of Hagar's fruitfulness made Sarah more embittered over her barrenness. The rivalry became so intense that finally Hagar fled from Sarah's abuse. Out in the desert the Angel of the Lord came to Hagar, and convinced her to go back to Sarah, and submit to her. This, no doubt, was not easy, but the Angel promised Hagar that she would have a son named Ishmael (God hears) and that:

He will be a wild donkey of a man; his hand will be against everyone and everyone's hand against him, and he will live in hostility toward all his brothers.

Genesis 16:12

So Hagar went back and gave birth to Ishmael. Abraham was 86 at the time, and assumed God's promises rested upon Ishmael. However, Ishmael was not the promised child being the child of unfaith, and not of faith in God's promises.

Fourteen years later, Isaac was born to Sarah and Abraham. Abraham was now 100 years young, and Sarah a sprightly 90. It is obvious that this was a miracle birth. The name Isaac means "laughter"—which could be due to two things: (1) Sarah laughed when she overheard the angels tell Abraham that she [Sarah] would yet have a son [at her age]. (2) When Isaac was born he brought joy and laughter back into the tents of Abraham (Genesis 21:6).

But the rivalry and jealousy between Sarah and Hagar continued—now through their children. Ishmael was 13 or 14 when Abraham threw a big feast or party for young Isaac. Ishmael, taking a lesson from the two mothers, was jealous and mocked Isaac. Upon seeing this, Sarah stirred up another desert storm demanding that Hagar and her son Ishmael be thrown out of the camp. She used strong words suggesting:

(Ishmael) will never share in the inheritance with my son Isaac.

Genesis 21:10

Abraham was distressed, being the father of both, and probably realized what a royal mess he'd created by trying to run ahead of God. However, God takes our failures and yet accomplishes His will. In the midst of this storm God consoled Abraham, and said to him:

Listen to whatever Sarah tells you, because it is through Isaac that your offspring will be reckoned. I will make the son of the maidservant into a nation also, because he is your offspring.

Genesis 21:12-13

So Hagar and Ishmael went out from the camp, and eventually Ishmael married an Egyptian girl. Ishmael became the father of the Arab nations, and Isaac the father of the Hebrews (or Jews). Abraham was the father of both nations. The rivalry that began in the camp of Abraham has spilled out over the centuries, even to this present day, upon the sands of the Middle East. It will eventually lead to Armageddon. God saw this in the beginning and allowed it to develop, for out of it, His will would be accomplished. God is the calm in the eye of the storm.

The Winds Of War

The winds of war have swept over Israel so many times that it is a miracle to see a Jew alive today. From the time of Abraham one desert storm after another has swirled around the Jew. Their lot in life has been a quest for survival. Yet, remarkably, and of course with God's help, they have survived.

27

In 1984 I visited Israel. About 2½ miles from the western shore of the Dead Sea, in the wilderness of Judea stands the rock fortress of Masada. Masada is 1,300 feet up overlooking the Dead Sea, with the top being ½ mile long and 220 yards wide. Masada has become a shrine for the Jews since it has been the site of one of the most dramatic episodes of Jewish history. It is the symbol of courage and heroism, the symbol of choice of death over slavery. In 40 B.C. Herod the Great built a huge, magnificent fortress at the top of Masada. After the destruction of Jerusalem in A.D. 70, a band of Jewish patriots led by Eleazar Ben Yair marched on Masada and captured it from a Roman garrison. Joined later by a few surviving patriots who evaded capture in Jerusalem, they determined to continue the fight for freedom and made Masada a base for guerrilla strikes against the Romans. In A.D. 72 Silva, a general of Titus, took the 10th legion, and marched on the great rock of Masada. Silva used traditional Roman siege techniques. A series of camps was established around the foot of the great rock, so that there was total encirclement. At the western side of the fortress, using thousands of Jewish slaves, he built a ramp of rocks and beaten earth. On this ramp he established a siege-tower and used this for covering fire to enable a battering-ram to be employed against the wall of the citadel. There were 960 men, women, and children in the citadel and the leader of the rebel defenders, Ben Yair, urged them to consider death rather than servitude. The Jews had a saying: "We are born that we may die and die that we may live." So the people took their own lives, first drawing lots to decide who should be the executioners. When the Romans breached the wall they found an awesome silence— 953 people dead with only two women and five small children alive to tell the story! The Roman victory was a hollow victory. A guide told me on the top of Masada that every Israeli today is sworn into the military with the words: "No more Masada!"[11]

Unfortunately, Masada was just one incident among many over the centuries affecting the Jewish quest for survival. The seed of Abraham has been scattered by the winds of war throughout history. Many of these desert storms were a result of the bitterness between the seed of Isaac and the seed of Ishmael. The following is a brief list of the trials that have befallen Israel through the centuries:

- **1227 B.C.**—The Great Exodus from Egypt. According to some authorities the date was about 1445 B.C. Moses, a stupendous figure, welded the jealous tribes into a people. He inculcated a purer idea of monotheism. He laid down the basis of an advanced moral and ethical system. He promulgated a code of laws (resting upon the 10 Commandments) which has formed the foundation of Jewish practice and jurisprudence to our own day, as well as much of the humanitarian idealism of modern times.[12]

- **721 B.C.**—Assyrians swept the ten northern tribes into captivity.

- **605 B.C.**—King Nebuchadnezzar of Babylon conquers Jerusalem.

- **586 B.C.**—Babylonian armies devastate Jerusalem and haul the Israelites to captivity in Babylon (modern day Iraq).

- **516 B.C.**—Under Ezra approximately 50,000 exiles return and rebuild the temple in Jerusalem. The city would not be rebuilt until after 445 B.C.

- **A.D. 70**—The Romans destroy the temple and Jerusalem—the temple has never been rebuilt. Today the "Dome of the Rock," a Muslim Mosque stands on the sacred area in Jerusalem. The Dome, known as the Mosque of Omar, was built at the end of the 7th century, by Caliph Abd el Malik Ben Merwan. Merwan, wanting to make Jerusalem a place of Muslim devotion instead of Mecca, built a splendid mosque spending all the taxes of his province (Egypt) for seven years on its construction. The mosque ranks in sanctity after that of the Kaaba and the tomb of the prophet in Medina, and is the oldest and most exquisite Muslim shrine in the world. The exterior is a rectangular octagon, each side measuring 63 feet with a diameter of 180 feet. Above it rises a dome on a cylindrical drum to a height of 108 feet from the ground, this has a diameter of 78 feet. The dome made of special aluminum bronze alloy shines like gold under the brilliant sun of Jerusalem. The mosque, keeping its primitive outline, has been restored many times during the centuries. The biggest and last restoration began in 1958 and was completed in 1964.

- **8th Century**—Arabs control Palestine.

- **12th Century, Crusades**—Decade after decade brought tales of woe and death to the Jew. Hounded by successions of crusaders, restrictions of church councils, accusations of ritual murder and blasphemy, Jewish life at the opening of the 15th century was a poor, hopeless, broken thing. Where was the Jew to go? Half the countries of Europe had expelled the Jews and were ruthlessly persecuting them. Everywhere, there was war in the name of peace, hate in the name of love. Still, Jews turned to the Torah and their prayer-books, scanning the tear stained pages in vain for the consolation which the living world denied them. Even Martin Luther, early in his career, summed up the dreadful hypocrisy of the Church with characteristic sharpness: "Our fools, the popes, bishops, sophists, and monks, have hitherto conducted themselves towards the Jews in such a manner that he who was a good Christian would have preferred to be a Jew. And if I had been a Jew and had seen such blockheads and louts ruling and teaching Christianity, I would have become a swine rather than a Christian, because they have treated the Jew like dogs, and not like human beings."[13]

- **1517**—The Ottoman Turks take control of the land.

- **1917**—General Allenby conquers Jerusalem and British occupation ensues. A landmark battle was fought at Megiddo overlooking the Valley of Megiddo or Armageddon. It was here that General Allenby defeated the Turkish army. In consequence of his victory, General Allenby received in England the honorary title "Lord of Aramageddon."[14]

- **1917, November 2, Balfour Declaration,** —Established a national home for Jewish people, but immediate pressure from the Arab world prevented fulfillment of this Declaration.

- **1939**—World War II breaks out and Hitler kills over 6,000,000 Jews. The magnitude of this Holocaust was not discovered until war's end.

- **1948, May 14**—Israel is declared an independent state following World War II. 5,000 square miles was assigned to the infant state which included about 650,000 Jews and hundreds of thousands of Arabs. This recognition of Israel was unacceptable to the Arab world and almost immediately Israel was attacked by Egypt, Jordan, Syria, Lebanon, Iraq, and Saudi Arabia. Israel won, extending its borders to around 8,000 square miles which included much of the Negev desert to the south.

- **1967**—Famous 6-day War. Sensing an attack, Israel struck first at Syrian, Jordanian, and Egyptian bases, totally defeating them and expanding its territory by 200%. At the cease fire, Israel now held the Golan Heights, the West Bank of the Jordan River, the Old City (Jerusalem), and all of the Sinai and east bank of the Suez Canal.

- **1973**—War erupts again on Yom Kippur, October 6, 1973, with a surprise Egyptian and Syrian assault on the Jewish high holy day. Two weeks later when a cease fire was initiated, all gains of the Syrian and Egyptian forces had been reversed. However, Israel suffered heavy losses in the war.

- **1978**—Israel retaliates against PLO attacks by invading Lebanon to attack PLO bases. Israel withdrew three months later turning over strongholds to the Lebanese Christian Militia.

- **1979**—Presidents Carter (U.S.A.), Begin (Israel), and Sadat (Egypt) signed historic peace treaty. Israel withdrew from Sinai on May 25th.

- **1981**—Israel bombed an Iraqi nuclear reactor on June 7th.

- **1982**—In retaliation of PLO assassination attempt on the Israeli Ambassador to London, Israel invaded Lebanon and drove the PLO to Beirut. 5,000 PLO's were believed trapped, but a truce was negotiated after world wide Arab protests and Israel withdrew.

■ **1990 Persian Gulf War**—37 Scud missile attacks by Iraq but Israel has not retaliated as of this writing. Israel was not a member of the Coalition Forces making up Desert Storm. Saddam Hussein was hoping by the attacks to split the Western/Arab alliance by drawing Israel into the war. It did not work as Israel exercised unusual patience at the urging of President Bush.

These historical events represented immense suffering to the Jew. Out of the twenty, three hold special Biblical significance, which will be discussed in detail later. They are:

1. A.D. 70 —The destruction of Jerusalem, end of the temple, and eventually building of the Mosque of Omar.

2. 1939—The Holocaust when Hitler killed 6,000,000 Jews.

3. 1967—The famous 6-day War and recapture of the old city of Jerusalem.

After reviewing the centuries of scattering and regathering of the Jew one wonders how flesh and blood could survive such trials. And keep in mind that these trials were not for years, nor decades, but centuries of unremitting woe, with more to follow. The Jews, however, seem to have remarkable powers of adjustment. When they suffered an apparently crushing calamity, they turned submissively to God to thank him for all that they might have borne, but had mercifully escaped! But perhaps the greatest reason for their survival is because God is a God of His Word. For He said to Abraham:

*I will establish my covenant as an **everlasting covenant** between me and you and your descendants after you for the generations to come . . .*

Genesis 17:7

GREAT EVENTS TIME CHART

	32 A.D.	Calvary
	70 A.D.	Fall of Jerusalem and Temple
Tribulation Period	688 A.D.	Dome of the Rock
	732 A.D.	Battle of Tours
	1939	Hitler and Nazi Germany
	1948	Rebirth of Israel
	1967	*Recapture Old City and End of Gentile Domination
End Times	?	**Second Coming**

* "Never again will we be driven from this place."

The Grinding Mills Of God

Israel and Iran (ancient Persia) have emerged from the recent war looking better than ever. Iran has an additional 137 fighter jets, plus the possibility of sole leadership among the Arab nations with the potential fall of Iraq. Regardless of who takes the reign of leadership in Iraq, it will take a while to regain all she has lost in the war. Israel, meanwhile, has been promised aid from the U.S. in the form of $160 million, plus now has the addition of Patriot Missiles (anti-missile missile) on her soil. And for the first time U.S. troops are there—at least for a time, with the Patriot launchers. This is all quite historical and apparently a prelude to Armageddon!

Eight Arab nations that lined up with the U.S. against Iraq have now united behind President Bush's call for an end to the Arab-Israeli conflict. Secretary of State James Baker went to Israel urging the Jewish State to compromise and match the Arab nations in a new willingness to pursue peace in the Middle East.

In the wake of the Gulf War it seems obvious that God has set the stage for the final events surrounding Israel. God's mills grind slowly but they do grind, as God used this war to finally fulfill Jeremiah's prophecies against Babylon (modern day Iraq). God ordained that Babylon would fall, and fall she did to the Medo-Persians. God has often used nations to punish other nations for their sins. Cyrus entered Babylon on October 29, 539 B.C. and presented himself in the role of liberator of the people. The gates had been opened to him without resistance. Although Jeremiah had predicted Babylon's downfall, the devastation predicted did not take place, as the city was left intact, and Cyrus instituted a kindly policy of repatriation for captive peoples.

Jeremiah 51 definitely predicted the coming of Cyrus and

the Persians as Babylon was responsible for the killing and deportation of thousands of God's people, as well as the pillage and plunder of the temple treasury. But the destructive parts of Jeremiah's prophecy remained basically unfulfilled until today.

Remember, God promised Abraham that He would *curse those who curse him* (Genesis 12:2-3). Saddam Hussein fired Scud missiles on Tel Aviv, and vowed to "annihilate Israel." No nation in the history of the annals of war has ever experienced the rain of devastation poured upon Iraq.

> *The sea will rise over Babylon; its roaring waves will cover her . . .*
>
> Jeremiah 51:42

Wave after wave of airplanes, like hords of locusts, filled the air above Iraq. By the time of the ground war assault, the Coalition forces were actually being slowed in their lightening attacks by hords of surrendering EPW's (Enemy Prisoners of War). Over 50,000 Iraqi soldiers were waving white flags of surrender. Some were actually parking their tanks and giving up to the Coalition forces. One officer was asked by an EPW, "What took you guys so long?" He wore a Chicago Bulls T-shirt! Even the vaunted Republican Guard was involved. I believe these unusual events are in fulfillment of Jeremiah's words:

> *Babylon's (Iraq's) warriors have stopped fighting; they remain in their strongholds (bunkers). Their strength is exhausted; they have become like women . . .*
>
> Jeremiah 51:30

There seems to be nothing in history to compare with these apocalyptic-like events of the Gulf War.

Perhaps these last events witnessed by millions on CNN, of the missile attacks and patience of Israel, will be the catalyst

God uses to return His people to the promised land. Time will tell.

Report 3

BACK TO THE FUTURE

T HREE major historical events have occurred over the centuries according to God's leading. These events, I believe, were predetermined and are major signposts pointing the way to His imminent return. In "Report Two—Israel" I briefly touched upon these three events. Each of these events were prophetically announced, and although historically fulfilled, will yet play a significant role in our future. Now I would like to elaborate more fully on these three historical events in relation to prophecy. They play a lead role in today's current events, and the future of the world.

Under The Influence

To know where we are going, there are a couple of technical matters we need to address first. Both the Old and New Testaments relate God's love message to fallen man. What is contained in the old is explained in the new. What is

39

concealed in the old is revealed in the new. The entire Bible is important to us. We are told:

> *All scripture is God-breathed and is useful for teaching, rebuking, correcting and training in righteousness.*
>
> II Timothy 3:16

The phrase "God-breathed" was originally translated "inspired." The question is immediately raised, "How were these men inspired to write the scriptures?" The scripture gives the answer—they were moved by the Holy Spirit (II Peter 1:21). In other words, they were under the influence of the Holy Spirit when they wrote. One might say they were "WUI— Writing Under the Influence." Often times they did not understand what they were writing or prophesying, since it was futuristic in nature.

Scripture was given mostly through the Prophets, and later the Apostles, over a 1,600 year period of time. The Old Testament was written in Hebrew and the New Testament in Greek. All versions of the Bible today, including the revered King James, were translated from the original manuscripts as best as possible. The truth is, we have a more accurate rendering of the Word today than we had when the King James was translated (1611). The old rendering of the King James Version, however archaic it's wording, still is the most beautiful and poetic. I do all my memory work from the King James since that is the book I "cut my teeth" on in the beginning of my spiritual journey.

God's plan, as revealed in the Bible, embraces many writing styles—prose, poetry, literal, and figurative. Much of the figurative consists of allegories and visions. Jesus used a lot of parables (story telling) in His teachings. Some people mistakenly interpret the entire Word as literal. This, of course, would present a lot of problems in interpretation.

BACK TO THE FUTURE

Actually, only a small portion of the Bible is figurative. However, this small portion is significant in that it includes what we often refer to as apocalyptic writings, i.e., writings that adopt a visionary or symbolic style. Writers such as Daniel, Ezekiel, and Zechariah have major apocalyptic passages. The Revelation, written by the apostle John, is practically all apocalyptic in nature.

To prevent further additions to the Word, the Holy Spirit moved John to write these words at the very end of his Revelation:

> *I warn everyone who hears the words of the prophecy of this book: If anyone adds anything to them, God will add to him the plagues described in this book. And if anyone takes words away from this book of prophecy, God will take away from him his share in the tree of life and in the holy city, which are described in this book.*
>
> Revelation 22:18-19

The warning is clear, and any reader will quickly discover there are a lot of plagues mentioned in the Book. So writers and editors beware!

The Day-Year Formula

It is clear to every student of the Word that there is a time element in the scriptures. We come across such divisions of time as "hours," "days," "weeks," "months," "years," "times," and "half a time." It is obvious that to avoid confusion all references to time must be interpreted on a similar scale, or with the same formula, as given in Numbers 14:34:

> *For forty years—one year for each of the forty days you explored the land—you will suffer for your sins and know what it is like to have me against you.*

41

Also the prophet Ezekiel said:

> *I have assigned you the same number of days as the years of their sin. So for 390 days you will bear the sin of the house of Israel. After you have finished this, lie down again, this time on your right side, and bear the sin of the house of Judah. I have assigned you 40 days, a day for each year.*
>
> Ezekiel 4:5-6

The Lord's formula then is, **One Day Stands For One Year.** In order to understand this formula we must first understand that there are years of different lengths. The Lunar Year has 354 days. The Calendar Year has 360 days. The Solar Year has 365 days. The Julian, or Astronomical Year has 365¼ days, making it necessary to add one day every 4 years to the calendar.

Now, which of these years can we use in our formula? We find the key in the Word of God. In Genesis 7:11-24 and 8:3-4, in the account of the Genesis Flood we discover that 5 months from the 17th day of the 2nd month, are reckoned as 150 days, or 30 days in a month, or 360 days in a year! So, we see according to prophetic chronology we are to use a Calendar year of 360 days. Let's see if it works.

In the 9th chapter of Daniel, the prophet had an unusual vision of "70 Weeks." Actually it reads:

> *Seventy sevens (or weeks) are decreed for your people and your holy city to finish transgression . . .*
>
> Daniel 9:24

Daniel had been in prayer as he knew that the 70 years of captivity in Babylon were coming to an end. He was concerned as to the future of his people. Daniel's prayer was interrupted by the angel Gabriel. The purpose of Gabriel's visit was to show Daniel that while his people would be restored to their own land at the end of the "70 Years" there would be a new and different "seventy sevens."

> *Seventy sevens are decreed for your people and your holy city to finish transgression, to put an end to sin, to atone for wickedness, to bring in everlasting righteousness, to seal up vision and prophecy and to anoint the most holy. Know and understand this: From the issuing of the decree to restore and rebuild Jerusalem until the Annointed One, the ruler comes, there will be seven sevens, and sixty-two sevens. It will be rebuilt with streets and a trench, but in times of trouble. After the sixty-two sevens, the Anointed One will be cut off and will have nothing . . .*
>
> Daniel 9:24-26

This is a powerful prophecy. It is a prophecy relating to the Jews and Jerusalem. Verse 24 tells us the following things must take place:

- Finish the transgression;
- Put an end to sin;
- Atone for wickedness;
- Bring everlasting righteousness;
- Seal up the vision; and
- Anoint the Most Holy.

The time frame for all this is 7 weeks and 62 weeks, for a total of 69 weeks! Furthermore, the Messiah will be killed at the end of the 69 weeks. Now do you see the importance of this prophecy?

Going back to our original formula of a "Day = Year" and that these "weeks" are years of 360 days in length. Our problem is to find the historical date when these years began. Again, the Word does not leave us in doubt. Our text tells us:

Know and understand this: From the issuing of the decree
to restore and rebuild Jerusalem until the Anointed One,
the ruler comes, there will be seven and sixty-two sevens . . .
Daniel 9:25

If we can locate the *issuing of this decree to restore and*
rebuild Jerusalem then we can fix its date and have the terminus
from which the prophecy takes its course. That is a bit more
difficult since there were four decrees issued altogether by
Cyrus, Darius, and Artaxerxes, recorded in the Book of Ezra.
But these decrees without exception have to do with the
rebuilding of the Temple, not the city.

There is only one decree in Old Testament history that relates
to what Daniel is talking about. That decree is found in the
book of Nehemiah:

In the month of Nisan (March-April), *in the twentieth*
year of King Artaxerxes . . . If it pleases the king and if
your servant has found favor in his sight, let him send
me to the city in Judah where my fathers are buried so
that I can rebuild it . . . And because the gracious hand
of my God was upon me, the king granted my requests.
Nehemiah 2:1-8

It is no surprise to learn that this date is one of the best
known dates in history. Even the Encyclopedia Britannica sets
the date of Artaxerxes' accession as 465 B.C.; and therefore
his twentieth year would be 445 B.C. The month was Nisan,
and since no day was given, according to Jewish custom the
date would be understood as the first. Thus our calendar would
be March 14, 445 B.C. This is the beginning of the seventy
weeks prophecy.[15]

In order to find the end of the Sixty-nine weeks, we must
first reduce them to days using our formula.

Since we have 69 weeks of seven years each, each year of 360 days: 69 × 7 × 360 = 173,880 days. Beginning with March 14, 445 B.C., this number brings us exactly to April 6, 32 A.D. Or, although not as precise: 69 × 7 = 483 Hebrew years. Converting these Hebrew years into solar years of 365.24 days give 476 solar years (483 × .9857 = 476). From 445 B.C. to A.D. 32 is 476 years. (1 B.C. to A.D. 1 is only 1 year).

April 6, 32 A.D. is the end of the 69 weeks of Daniel. It prophetically marks the very day Jesus rode into Jerusalem on the "foal of an ass" and offered Himself as the Prince and King of Israel! Daniel's prophecy was truly "back to the future" since it was 173,880 days, or 476 years prior to the event. Indubitably, Daniel was a true prophet of God!

Thus Jesus fulfilled all five of the six points of Daniel 9:24:

(He) finished the transgression, put an end to sin, atoned for wickedness, brought everlasting righteousness, and was anointed the Most Holy.

All of these things He accomplished through His blood sacrifice. But He did not seal up the vision. So there is more.

God's Pet Rock

Centuries upon centuries ago, God instructed Abraham to take his promised son Isaac to a place called Mount Moriah. Abraham, in faith, was about to offer his favorite son Isaac (not Ishmael) as a blood sacrifice on Mount Moriah's rock. Instead, God provided a lamb for the sacrifice. This lamb was a foreshadow, or type of the Perfect Lamb to come two thousand years later. But in between, God would allow some important events to take place on His mountain.

Nearly a thousand years after Abraham, God had David purchase Mount Moriah from Ornan, who had built a threshing floor on that special place. David dreamed of building a temple there. His son Solomon followed David's blueprints and built the temple on this very summit where Abraham had taken Isaac. This was in 960 B.C. and 380 years later Nebuchadnezzar destroyed this temple, in 586 B.C. And the Jews, Daniel included, were carried into captivity to Babylon. Seventy years later, Ezra, with about 50,000 returning Jews rebuilt the temple, although it was not as glorious as Solomon's first temple. During the time of Jesus, King Herod engaged in a massive remodeling of the temple in hopes of appeasing the Jews. It involved 46 years (see John 2:20) and did not interfere with the services of worship. Since only the priests could enter the inner court, Herod enlisted 1,000 of the priests for masons and carpenters for that inner area.

In Matthew 24, Jesus issues an amazing prophecy. He predicts the total destruction of this marvelous temple and city.

I tell you the truth, not one stone here will be left on another; every one will be thrown down.

Matthew 24:2

The End Of The Temple

In A.D. 70, just as Jesus had predicted, the Romans, under Titus, totally destroyed Jerusalem and the temple. On the 9th day of Ab (July-August), almost the exact anniversary of the destruction of Jerusalem by Nebuchadnezzar the Temple was stormed and whether by accident or design committed to the flame.[16] Josephus says that over 1,000,000 perished in the four month siege, while 97,000 survived as captives and many of the young men were taken to Rome to work as slaves. Thus another fulfillment of Daniel that . . .

the people of the ruler will come and destroy the city and the sanctuary . . .
Daniel 9:26

Afterwards, except for a short lived temple of Jupiter, the mountain summit became a garbage dump. Then in A.D. 638, during the 1st Jihad (holy war) the Muslim Arabs took Jerusalem. Toward the end of the 7th century, Caliph Abd el Malik Ben Merwan constructed the "Dome of the Rock." As previously stated the mosque ranks in sanctity after that of the Kaaba and the tomb of the prophet in Medina. "The vein of bedrock that breaks into the open there, that stone from which Muslims believe Muhammad rose on his horse to heaven, may also be the *Even Shetiyah,* the rock around which the earth was created, according to ancient Jewish lore . . . "[17] To the Moslem world it is a precious Shrine. To the Jew an Abomination of Desolation. And it stands on God's sacred mountain today.

The Abomination Of Desolation

The Babylonian Empire had fallen to Cyrus the Persian. Daniel, now in his old age, receives a final prophecy about his people. He had been held captive for over 73 years by the time he received this vision. It is recorded in Daniel chapter twelve:

From the time that the daily sacrifice is abolished and the abomination that causes desolation is set up, there will be 1,290 days. Blessed is the one who waits for and reaches the end of the 1,335 days.
Daniel 12:11-12

What exactly does the phrase "abomination of desolation" mean? First, it involves the temple area. Most scholars agree that in 165 B.C., Antiochus Epiphanes created an abominable act when he sacrificed a pig on the temple altar, and forced some of the Jews to eat pork. That has become known as a "type" of the abomination to come. Apparently it will be either an idol on the temple grounds or some unclean abominable sacrifice. It occurs after the abolition of sacrifices . . . "at a time when the daily sacrifice is abolished . . . " There is absolutely no reason to assume that the Lord is giving Daniel instructions about some abolition of sacrifices to come in the Christian era. Christ ended the need for all such sacrifices! When he died on the cross the temple veil was split in two—that ended the need for further sacrifices. To get the Jews to stop sacrificing he had to literally destroy the temple in A.D. 70.

Sacrifices were ended at least three times in the Old Testament. Nebuchadnezzar destroyed the temple in 586 B.C. but Jeremiah tells us that sacrifices continued (Jeremiah 41:5). These sacrifices apparently took place under the Governorship of Gedeliah, ten months after the destruction of the temple! Nebuchadnezzar ascended the throne in 606 B.C. Twenty-three years later, in 583 B.C. he hauled off more captives from Jerusalem. Jeremiah claims about 4,600. Included in this group was 745 (Jeremiah 52:30). This significance of this small sub-group is that they probably were priests who remained in the land carrying on the sacrificial rituals. This would be important to Daniel and Jeremiah.[18] When Daniel heard the final prophecy of 1,290 years, and noted that it would be after the abolition of sacrifices. So he used the day-year formula advocated by Ezekiel (Ezekiel 4:5-6) and Moses (Numbers 14:34), and as previously discussed. He looked down the road from 583 B.C. for 1,290 years to the abomination of desolation. What did he see?

1290 Hebrew Years (1271.5 solar years) – 583 B.C. = A.D. 688.5

688.5 years had passed since the abolition of sacrifices.

What took place in A.D. 688 that would be so significant to Daniel's people? In history we know that it was the year the Caliph built the **Dome of the Rock.** (The Academic American Encyclopedia, Vol. I-J p. 401, tells us that the Arab Muslims took Jerusalem in A.D. 638. They began construction on the Dome of the Rock in A.D. 688. Construction lasted until A.D. 691) Therefore, the Dome of the Rock is the Abomination of Desolation on God's mountain! Mark seems to confirm this as he refers to the "abomination" as an "it" and not a "he" (Mark 13:14). The Dome is a Mosque, an abomination to the Jew and to God—it is an abominable "it."

The Temple Mount is a raised, flat area of about 175,000 square yards just inside, and bordered by, the eastern wall of the Old City, facing Gethsemane and the Mount of Olives. Today, it is a place of sacred conjunction for both Islam and Judaism.

The western wall, or wailing wall as it is known, is the main focus of Jewish worship, but only out of frustration. This wall is nothing more than a massive retaining wall holding up the Temple Mount. In a sense, prayer there is a lamentation for the Second Temple, which has never been replaced since being burned by the Romans in A.D. 70.

The Dome Of The Spirits

The significant thing to remember about all this is that the Caliph ordered the "Dome of the Rock," to be built on the wrong spot. Jewish scholars can show you the exact place of the Holy of Holies, and where the 2nd Temple stood—and it is not where the Dome of the Rock stands!

Some 300 feet north of the Dome of the Rock stands an unimposing "Dome of the Spirits." Sometimes called "Dome of the Tablets." It is located exactly on an East to West line with the Golden Gate and is where the Ark of the Covenant rested. For this very reason, since 1967, the Jews were proscribed by the chief rabbis even from setting foot on the Temple Mount, lest they inadvertantly step into the area once occupied by the Holy of Holies, that chamber of the temple into which only the high priests, having been properly purified, could go. Some religious zealots have ignored this injunction as they sought to pray on that sacred spot. One young Jew proudly boasted that he snuck past the guards and became the first Jew in 2,000 years to blow the Shofar, or ritual ram's horn, on the Temple Mount. He blew it and ran!

The fascinating thing about all this is that scripture predicted the Dome of the Rock would be built on the wrong spot. Listen to what John says in Revelation:

> *I was given a reed like a measuring rod and was told, Go and measure the temple of God and the altar, and count the worshipers there. But exclude the outer court; do not measure it, because it has been given to the Gentiles. They will trample on the holy city for 42 months.*
>
> Revelation 11:1-2

God ordained that the Caliph would build on the wrong spot! Perhaps a more accurate theological statement is, God allowed them to build right where He wanted them to build—on the court of the Gentiles.

Notice the words, *exclude the outer court; do not measure it, because it has been given to the Gentiles . . .* For a long time we could not understand this statement. Now we know what it means. The Dome of the Rock, an infamous Gentile structure, is built over the "Court of the Gentiles!"

Additional proof is offered by the injunction that *they will trample on the city for 42 months.* Remember, a solar year is 365.24 days. There are 12 months in a year, thus each month contains 30.44 days. $42 \times 30.44 = 1278.5$ days, (Don't forget the Day = Year Formula.) After the war of 1948, the

Jews held west Jerusalem only. East Jerusalem, with the old city containing the western wall and the Temple Mount, was in Jordanian hands. An ugly barrier of barbed wire and stone separated the Israeli and Jordanian zones, cutting through the heart of Jerusalem until the 1967 war. Then, Jordan, along with other Arab states attacked Israel. However, Israel fought back and captured **all** the territory from its eastern border to the Jordan River. That gave the Israelis the West Bank, the Old City, and the Temple Mount![19]

There on June 6, 1967, the Jews stood crying and praying at the Wailing Wall for the first time. They swore: "Never again will we be driven from this place." And that brings us back to the 42 months of Revelation:

1967 – 1278.5 solar years = A.D. 688
(Construction began on the Dome of the Rock.)

Let's recap: We have now seen the consistency of both the Old Testament and the New Testament. Daniel looked forward into time 1290 Hebrew years to the construction of the Dome, whereas John looks back in time 42 months or 1278 solar years. Both arrive at the same date in history, A.D. 688. Scanning the centuries then, we find these results:

1. Old Testament: Daniel looks forward in time.

   583 B.C. + 1271 = A.D. 688
   Note: 1290 Hebrew years are 1271 Solar years. 583 B.C. was the year of abolition of sacrifices. A.D. 688 was when the Dome's construction began, (Daniel 12:11-12).

2. New Testament: John looks back in time.

   1967 – 1278 = 688
   Note: 1967 is the date the Jews recaptured the Old City and the Temple Mount, ending Gentile domination. 1278 are solar years of 42 months (Revelation 11:1-2).

A Nation Born Again!

Everyone knows by now that the nation of Israel was "born again" in 1948. On May 14, 1948 the British troops left Palestine. At midnight the new Jewish state, called Israel, was officially born again. Eleven minutes later the State was recognized by the United States, and two days later by Russia. At the same time, the armies of Syria, Lebanon, Egypt, Iraq, and Transjordan crossed into the new state and attacked Jewish settlements.[20] Was this date, 1948, predicted in Scripture?

Indirectly, it was. Daniel had his vision in 536 B.C. Daniel was told there would be seven sevens, and sixty-two sevens, and a final seven. We have already looked at this "70 weeks." Does this final week have anything to do with the rebirth of Israel?

If we use our day = year formula we discover:

$360 \times 7 = 2520$ days, or 2484 solar days.

Now we can see what we have from the time of Daniel's vision:

2484 − 536 B.C. = A.D. 1948—The Birth of Israel.[21]

Hitler And The Third Reich

In the seventh chapter of Daniel the prophet had a dream. He dreamed he saw four voracious beasts coming up out of the sea (from among the nations). Daniel saw:

(1) A lion with wings of an eagle;

(2) A bear;

(3) A leopard;

(4) A terrible beast (like one from a Stephen King novel), with iron teeth and ten horns.

Back To The Future

These beasts were prophetic in nature representing Gentile world powers to come. Out of the ten horns of the final terrible beast came a "little horn." This little horn waged war and spoke great things, (Note: this little horn is not the same as the little horn of Daniel 8). He came out of the Roman Empire, or the last of the great world empires. In 1933 Adolf Hitler came to power. He re-established the Roman Empire and waged war on the Jew. In the summer of 1941 final plans were laid for the extermination of the Jew. The process was carried out by the Gestapo, or German secret police. In the course of the next few months reports began to filter out to the western world of the horrors of the death camps at Majdanek, Treblinka, Auschwitz, etc. Jewish people were being round-up and deported to these camps for extermination by the thousands and scores of thousands—by shooting, by injections, and above all, by poison gas. It is hardly possible for the human mind to grasp the scale of heartless atrocities which took place, in the twentieth century, at the hands of ostensibly civilized people. In Birkenou alone, more than 1,750,000 Jews were murdered within two years.[22]

Nazi Germany, under Hitler's leadership, subdued almost all of the old geographic Roman Empire, and like other empires of history had beast-like qualities. This Third Reich (or 3rd Roman Empire) was supposed to last 1000 years. It lasted 12 years . . . *A little season* as Revelation 17:10 tells us. This little horn came out of the Roman Empire, and Hitler was the last of its emperors. It is obvious to all by now that no dictator in the history of the entire world has possessed more beast-like qualities than Hitler. Hitler was solely responsible for the slaughter of millions of the seed of Abraham.

I am indebted to E.H. Skolfield for his comparison of the Roman Empire with the Nazi German Empire under Hitler:

THE BEAST OF THE EAST

Roman Empire	German Empire
1. The Roman Eagles	The German Eagles
2. The Roman Legions	The German Legions
3. Hail Caesar	Heil Hitler
4. Caesar Worshipped	Hitler Diefied
5. Military State	Military State
6. War Glorified	War Glorified
7. Great Public Works	Great Public Works
8. Thousands Killed	Millions Slaughtered

This little horn (Hitler) had to come before 1948, while the Jews were still among the nations. Of all the conquerors in the Christian era, Hitler had the greatest impact. He was responsible for the killing of 6,000,000 Jews! The nations of the world had such guilt after World War II that they said: "The Jews must have their own home State." God used the holocaust, as evil as it was and Satanically inspired, to establish a State for the Jews. That is why Daniel was shown this vision. The Little Horn of Daniel 7 covers the same period of time as John's vision in Revelation 17. There we read:

The beast which you saw, once was, now is not, and will come up out of the Abyss and go to his destruction. The inhabitants of the earth . . . will be astonished when they see the beast, because he once was, now is not, and yet will come . . . Five have fallen, one is, the other has not yet come; but when he does come, he must remain for a little while. The beast who once was, and now is not, is an eighth king. He belongs to the seven and is going to his destruction.
Revelation 17:8-11

54

BACK TO THE FUTURE

John, like the prophet Daniel, receives a Beastly vision of the world empires, in contrast to Wealth and Might as seen by Nebuchadnezzar in his dream (Daniel 2). The King of Babylon dreamed of four great empires, but John's vision goes back further in history to the first great empire—Egypt.

According to our passage (Revelation 17), we can list these empires as follows:

- Five Empires That Are History
    - (1) **Egypt**
    - (2) **Assyria**
    - (3) **Babylon**—Lion
    - (4) **Medo-Persia**—Bear
    - (5) **Greece**—Leopard
- The Present Empire (at the time of John's Vision)
    - (6) **Rome**—Terrible Beast
- The Empire (or Beast) to come will be out of the Roman Empire and in John's future, and will last only a short while.
    - (7) **Nazi Germany** under Adolph Hitler
- The Eighth Empire (or Beast) to come. This beast was of the seven, and apparently will make a come back before destruction.
    - (8) ???

After this prophecy, Daniel has little to say about Rome, or the western empires. The reason being, the Jews are back in their homeland—since 1948—and Europe will no longer play a major role in God's plans for His people. Our attention will shift to the Middle East . . . to the Lion, Bear, and Leopard.

Report 4

BEASTLY EMPIRES

BEFORE we go to the lion/bear/leopard-like beast we need to go back to Daniel, and look again at these beastly empires. That way, we can see exactly in what direction the world is headed, and we will not be surprised when the sands shift toward Armageddon.

The Failure Of Quacks

In the second year of Nebuchadnezzar's reign he had a dream. The King summoned all his astrologers, magicians, and sorcerers (who used drugs) to tell him the dream and the interpretation. After all, they were making fortunes from the Babylonians with their astrological charts and "Dear Abu Akbar" columns. But, of course, these quacks could not even begin to relate the King's dream to him. Daniel, a young Hebrew prophet of God, serving in the King's court was brought before Nebuchadnezzar. It is interesting to note that no matter what the circumstances, God always has someone available to serve Him. Here in the great city of Babylon, with it's historical hanging gardens, God appropriately placed Daniel. Daniel's interpretation of the King's dream was eschatological in nature. It affected Nebuchadnezzar and our present day world.

The King dreamed that he saw a large statue (Daniel 2:31-48). The statue's head was gold, chest and arms silver, belly and thighs bronze, legs iron, feet iron with clay. Suddenly, a rock was cut from a mountain (not by human hands) and smashed the statue in the feet. The entire statue was broken in pieces and crumbled to the floor like dust (or wheat chaff) which the wind swept away. The rock then grew into a mighty mountain and filled the earth.

Daniel interpreted this to be a vision of Gentile world powers, starting with Nebuchadnezzar of Babylon. Notice also the descendancy of precious commodities in the dream: Gold, silver, bronze, iron, and clay.

Interpretation

You O King, Daniel said, *are the head of Gold.* Nebuchadnezzar was like a king of kings—an absolute monarch. He ruled the greatest power (kingdom) on earth. And God had used Babylon to punish Israel for her sins. But God would eventually punish Babylon for her sins according to Jeremiah 50 & 51. We saw the long range fulfillment of this in the recent Gulf War.

Daniel explained that there would be four major Gentile world powers, in order:

> (1) Babylon
>
> (2) Medo-Persia
>
> (3) Greece
>
> (4) Rome

The fifth power would be out of the Roman Empire (from the feet and toes) . . . a sort of revival of the Roman Empire. We've already discussed how Nazi Germany was that revival under Hitler, and the similar comparisons of those two empires.

King Nebuchadnezzar was so struck by the interpretation that he did what any egotistical monarch would do: he ordered a 90 foot statue built—of gold. And it was set up in the plain of Dura. The statue was probably an image of the King himself. The next step was to order the people to worship the golden image, for Nebuchadnezzar had begun to think of himself as a god.

Daniel's Dream

Now it is Daniel's turn. In the seventh chapter of Daniel the prophet has a dream. It is a continuation of the dream that God originally gave to Nebuchadnezzar, only from a different perspective. God's perspective.

Daniel dreamed he saw four voracious beasts coming up out of the sea (from among the nations). They were in order:

(1) A lion with the wings of an eagle

(2) A bear

(3) A leopard

(4) A terrible beast (like one from a horror story) with iron teeth and ten horns

The beasts represented the same Gentile world powers that Nebuchadnezzar had formerly dreamed about. Only Nebuchadnezzar's dream was from man's perspective . . . gold, silver, bronze, iron, and clay. Man sees world kingdoms as something precious to be desired, but God sees them as beasts devouring one another! For in Daniel's dream he saw the lion, bear, leopard, and terrible beast.

This dream, like Nebuchadnezzar's was prophetic and eschatological in nature. It reiterates that there will be four major Gentile world empires and that the fifth would eventually come out of the fourth. Overlapping the two dreams we get the following historical information:

1. **Babylonian Empire:**
   Characteristics: Like a lion and fashioned of gold. Nebuchadnezzar was an absolute monarch. His word was law. He was literally "king of the jungle." Gold represents deity and Nebuchadnezzar proclaimed himself as a god to be worshipped.

2. **Medo-Persian Empire:**
   Characteristics: Like a bear and fashioned of silver. This empire noted for its fierce countenance, like a bear that stands up on its hind feet and roars, producing fear and anguish in its victims. Silver represents redemption. The ancient tabernacle rested upon bars of silver in the sand, just as our salvation rests upon the blood sacrifice of Christ—redemption. Ironically, the fierce bear-like qualities of the Medo-Persian Empire also exhibited redemptive qualities. They did not destroy the historical and cultural beauty of Babylon, but more importantly, they acted redemptively toward the Jew, allowing them to return to their homeland.

3. **Grecian Empire:**
   Characteristics: Like a leopard and fashioned of bronze. Under Alexander the Great the Greeks swept the world overrunning one people after another. With weapons of bronze they were as swift as a leopard, and left a lasting influence throughout the ancient world.

The Four Beastly Empires of the Book of Daniel:

1. Babylonian: Like a Lion.
2. Medo-Persian: Like a Bear.

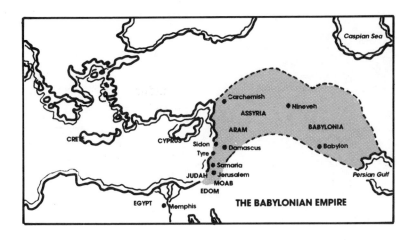

THE BABYLONIAN EMPIRE

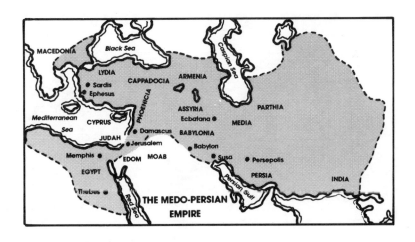

THE MEDO-PERSIAN EMPIRE

3. Grecian: Like a Leopard.
4. Roman: Like a Terrible Beast.

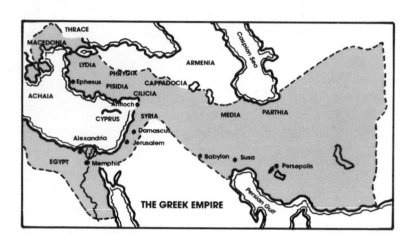

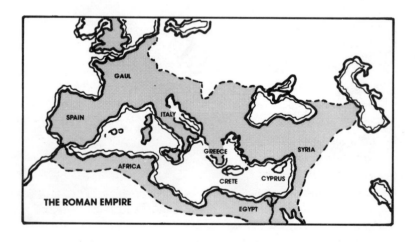

4. **Roman Empire:**
> Characteristics: Like a terrible beast fashioned of iron. The Romans were unconquerable—like iron. Their legions marched over the globe like a beast on a rampage. Nothing stood in their way as this beast with iron-like teeth crushed its victims. The Romans destroyed Jerusalem and the temple, and persecuted the Christian Church. Although filled with corruption and evil emperors, Rome never fell like the other empires. You could say it just "mellowed out," and the world woke up one morning to the western civilization.

The Scarlet Beast

Revelation 17 is probably one of the more difficult chapters in the entire Bible. Revelation 17 and 13 are overlapping chapters that follow closely the prophetic ideas of Daniel. These two chapters also continue the idea of beastly empires. So to be consistent with what we've already learned, it is necessary to follow that pattern of interpretation.

The best way to study Revelation 17 is to look at it in print.

> *One of the seven angels who had the seven bowls came and said to me, "Come, I will show you the punishment of the great prostitute, who sits on many waters. With her the kings of the earth committed adultery and the inhabitants of the earth were intoxicated with the wine of her adulteries." Then the angel carried me away in the Spirit into a desert. There I saw a woman sitting on a scarlet beast that was covered with blasphemous names and had seven heads and ten horns. The woman was dressed in purple and scarlet, and was glittering with gold, precious stones and pearls. She held a golden cup in her hand, filled with*

*abominable things and filth of her adulteries. This title was written on her forehead: **Mystery Babylon the Great the Mother of Prostitutes and of the Abominations of the Earth.** I saw that the woman was drunk with the blood of the saints, the blood of those who bore testimony to Jesus . . . The beast, which you saw, once was, now is not, and will come up out of the Abyss and go to his destruction . . . The seven heads are seven hills on which the woman sits. They are also seven kings. Five have fallen, one is, the other has not yet come; but when he does come, he must remain for a little while. The beast who once was, and now is not, is an eighth king. He belongs to the seven and is going to his destruction . . . The woman you saw is the great city that rules over the kings of the earth.*

Revelation 17:1-18

The woman, to John who is receiving this vision, is Babylon, that is to say, Rome. This chapter presents some complications but they can be easily explained. The woman in the passage is said to be sitting upon "many waters." John was really writing about the Roman Empire (to us the western world), but was using the code symbolism of "Babylon." In scripture "Babylon" is synonymous with evil. Literally, Babylon set on "many waters." The river Euphrates actually ran through the middle of the ancient city, and the canal or irrigation system spread out in every direction through the city. As John continues writing this chapter he changes that phrase, as he realizes it doesn't make sense to apply Babylon who sits on *many waters* to Rome who sits on *seven hills.* So, John makes the shift in verse 15 as he symbolically interprets:

The waters you saw, where the prostitute sits, are peoples, multitudes, nations, and languages.

In verse 4 the woman is said to be clothed in purple and scarlet and decked out with *gold, precious stones, and pearls.*

This is obviously the symbol of the wealth and luxury that existed in Rome in John's day. It is also a picture of how wealth is used to seduce the people of the earth. If the woman is symbolically Rome, then clearly the beast is the Roman Empire, full of blasphemous names. This fits with Daniel as Rome is a *terrible beast* in Daniel's dream. But let's move on further to see how it fits with Daniel's dream.

The *seven hilled* city was a standard description of Rome. This automatically identifies the beast with the imperial city and the empire of Rome. But John throws a riddle our way. He says:

> *The seven heads are seven hills on which the woman sits. They are also seven kings. Five have fallen, one is, the other has not yet come; but when he does come, he must remain for a little while. The beast who once was, and now is not, is an eighth king. He belongs to the seven and is going to his destruction.*
> Revelation 17:9-11

Historically, John could figure this out . . . to a point. Obviously he could not figure out the future, unless the angel gave him the full interpretation. Actually, we have a better shot at it because of past history.

Roman Emperors

Let's examine what John has told us, as John did— historically:

- *Five have fallen.*

  The first five emperors of the Roman Empire were: Augustus, Tiberius, Caligula, Claudius, and Nero. These then, are the five which have fallen. After the death of Nero there was confusion for two years and three emperors followed each other in quick succession.

- *One is.*

  Vespasian was on the throne from A.D. 69-79 and brought back stability to the throne. John would know this.

- *The other has not yet come, but when he does come he must remain for a little while.*

  John knew that Vespasian was succeeded by Titus. Titus reigned only two short years, from A.D. 79-81. So, historically, this fits well.

- *The beast who once was, and now is not, is an eighth king. He belongs to the seven, and is going to his destruction.*

  John was writing around A.D. 90 under the reign of Domitian. John might have identified Domitian as this "eighth king," or beast. There is the possibility that John saw in Domitian a reincarnation of the evil of Nero. Domitian was insane, evil, and dangerous. The Roman biographer, Suetonius wrote that Domitian "spent hours in seclusion every day, doing nothing but catching flies and stabbing them with a keenly-sharpened stylus." How would you like your President spending time in the White House doing that? As evil as Domitian was, John probably couldn't forget Nero, and neither could the Roman Empire. This is a clear reference to the *Nero redivivus*, or Nero resurrected legend that existed in John's day. According to the legend traveling throughout the Roman Empire, Nero was not really dead. He had been wounded, but escaped to Parthia in the east, and there he was waiting his time to return with the Parthian hordes to devastate and regain the throne.[23] This legend doesn't seem so ridiculous when one considers similar legends floating around today. Such as, Elvis is not dead, or John Kennedy still is alive and living in Poland, etc. In John's day, Nero, as evil as he was, was thought of as the Anti-christ and the legend simply enhanced this idea of evil incarnate! Now let's see how this all fits with Daniel.

The Big Picture

John, who was writing in exile, under the evil dominance of Rome, saw Rome as evil incarnate. And the emperor, especially Nero, was an Anti-christ. Martin Luther had similar feelings about the Pope in his day. But John, like Daniel, was really giving us a glimpse of the "big picture." It is amazing how God used the historical reigns of these Roman emperors, and all their evil, to parallel the evil beastly reigns of world empires. This is what we want to look at now in order to bring it all together, and keep in mind that Kings (Emperors) equals Empires.

Eight Major World Empires

- *Seven heads are seven hills . . . they are also seven kings. Five have fallen . . .* (Revelation 17:9-10)

    (1) **Egyptian Empire** (out of which Israel escaped).
        1st Roman Emperor—Augustus

    (2) **Assyrian Empire** (conquered Northern 10 Tribes).
        2nd Roman Emperor—Tiberius

    (3) **Babylonian Empire** (Lion)
        3rd Roman Emperor—Caligula

    (4) **Medo-Persian Empire** (Bear)
        4th Roman Emperor—Claudius

(5) **Grecian Empire** (Leopard)
5th Roman Emperor—Nero

■ *One is . . .* (Revelation 17:10)

(6) **Roman Empire** (Terrible Beast)
6th Roman Emperor—Vespasian

■ *The other is not yet come; but when he does come, he must remain for a little while.* (Revelation 17:10)

(7) **Hitler's Nazi German Empire** ("A little while")
7th Roman Emperor—Titus (reigned A.D. 79-81)

■ *The beast who once was, and now is not, is an eighth King. He belongs to the seven and is going to his destruction . . .* (Revelation 17:10)

(8) **Lion/Bear/Leopard Empire**—Led by Anti-christ.
8th Roman Emperor—Domitian.

The Seventh Beast

Since John was writing in A.D. 90, it was easy for him to see what we've seen up through Titus of the Roman Empire. However, he would not have known about Hitler. John could only speculate that a beast to come (the Seventh one) was to have an impact on his people for *a little while*, just as Titus lasted only a short while (A.D. 79-81). Actually Hitler lasted about 12 years although he boasted that the Third Reich would last for 1000 years. They were only 988 years off! The Seventh King (Hitler), although lasting only a short time, controlled most of Europe. He seized Poland, Yugoslavia, Greece, all of Northern Africa except for Egypt, and after Mussolini died, Italy. He practically re-established the Roman Empire! He was the *little horn* of Daniel 7, and the Seventh King (or Empire) of Revelation 17. I don't know why prophecy books tend to ignore Hitler, who reigned for a short while, but long enough to kill six million Jews. The Seventh beast was so vicious that after the war the United Nations knew they had to give the number one victim of the war—the Jew—a homeland. Prophetically then, the Seventh Beast produced in 1948 the end of Gentile domination of the Holy Land! The Jew was home again, and in control of his destiny, for the first time since Darius of 536 B.C., (A period of 2484 years!). Unfortunately, the Eighth Beast is to come . . . the one with Lion/Bear/Leopard-like qualities . . . and this beast will be the "Beast of the East."

THE BEAST OF THE EAST

JOHN'S PICTURE OF ANTI-CHRIST (BEASTS)

SCRIPTURE	BEAST	BEASTLY EMPIRE	EVENTS
Rev. 17:9-10 "5 Have Fallen"	1. Augustus 2. Tiberius 3. Caligula 4. Claudius 5. Nero	Rome Rome Rome Rome Rome	Persecution Persecution Persecution Persecution Persecution
"One Is"	6. Vespasian 67-79 A.D.	Rome	Destruction of Temple 70 A.D.
"A Little While"	7. Titus 79-81 A.D.	Rome	Persecution
	Hitler 1889- 1945 A.D.	Nazi 1935-45	WWII 8/6/45: Hiroshima 8/8/45: Nagasaki
"Out of Seven"	8. Domitian	Rome	Persecution
	Anti-christ ?	Lion, Bear Leopard	Armageddon ?

Report 5

THE BEAST OF THE EAST

I N the last report (Report Four), we learned that the final
beast (the eighth beast), would emerge from the previous
five fallen empires. We have already seen that Revelation
17 reveals a picture of the western world. Now, Revelation
13 will duplicate the picture, only it will be of the eastern
world. Or, from the empires that emerged from the Leopard,
Bear, and Lion. In other words, Revelation 13, gives us a
picture of the Beast of the East. And that's what I want to
look at now.

> *And I saw a beast coming out of the sea. He had ten
> horns and seven heads, with ten crowns on his horns, and
> on each head a blasphemous name. The beast I saw resem-
> bled a leopard, but had feet like those of a bear and a
> mouth like that of a lion. The dragon gave the beast his
> power and his throne and great authority.*
>
> Revelation 13:1-2

In order to remain consistent, keep in mind that each beast represents an empire. The beasts of Nebuchadnezzar and Daniel all represented empires that have come and gone. The seventh beast was Hitler and his revived Roman Empire. He lasted a *little while*. This eighth beast *once was,* and belonged *to the seven,* or, comes out of the seven, and he resembles parts of the Lion, Bear, and Leopard. Thus we have a clue as to what he is like. The Lion was Babylon, the Bear the Medo-Persian Empire, and the Leopard the Grecian Empire. This beast will resemble some of each of the three. These were middle eastern empires, not western empires like Rome. This eighth beast, therefore, will come from the Middle East. He will truly be the Beast of the East.

It is also obvious that this eighth beast to come, is from the heart or geographic center of the Islamic faith. The very people responsible for building the Dome of the Rock! Now do you see how this all ties together? Those responsible for the initial abomination of desolation will now descend upon the world one final time looking like a Lion, Bear, and Leopard!

The Woman In A Basket

Many scholars believe that Zechariah foretold the coming of the Islamic faith. Zechariah saw a woman in a basket. The woman, like the woman on the scarlet beast of Revelation 17, represented wickedness. When she tried to get out of the basket she was pushed back down, with a lid covering her. Then the basket was flown away. Zechariah asked,

Where are they taking the basket?

He was told,

To the country of Babylonia to build a house for it. When it is ready, the basket will be set there in its place.
Zechariah 5:5-11

72

The woman pictured here is symbolic of the organization described in Revelation Chapter 9, an organization which would change the face of the earth, and eventually give us the Beast of the East.

A Fallen Star

In the 9th chapter of Revelation we read:

The fifth angel sounded his trumpet, and I saw a star that had fallen from the sky to the earth. The star was given the key to the shaft of the Abyss. When he opened the Abyss, smoke rose from it like the smoke from a gigantic furnace. The sun and sky were darkened by the smoke from the Abyss. And out of the smoke locusts came down upon the earth and were given power like that of scorpions of the earth. They were told not to harm the grass of the earth or any plant or tree, but only those people who did not have the seal of God on their foreheads. They were not given power to kill them but only to torture them for five months.

Revelation 9:1-5

In this remarkable chapter a "star" fall from heaven, which is indicative of some mighty chieftain or leader, who is given the key to the bottomless pit. He opens the pit and allows swarms of locusts to go forth under a certain command:

To attack those who do not have the seal of God on their foreheads, and in their devastating attacks they are not to harm the earth.

How are we to understand such symbolism? The intent and purpose of the writer (John) is to reveal that this organization, described as locusts swarming, have ascended up from hell. The writer wants to make no mistake about it that this outfit has emitted from hell! And at the appropriate time, like the wicked woman in the basket, they embark upon their evil mission. The symbolism of locusts is definitely oriental. Locusts have a ravenous appetite and devour everything in their path. The locusts in this passage, therefore, represent an all-devouring army, an army which would be loosed for five months, or 150 days, or 150 years, since a day equals a year in scripture. As John wrote this passage he knew that the first four trumpets terminated with the downfall of the western empire, or Rome. The scene now changes, Rome has fallen, and a new power emerges from the East. With surprising unanimity, commentators agree that this passage refers to the empire of the Saracens, or the rise and power of the religion of Mohammed. The alleged prophet of Mecca, therefore, is the "star fallen from heaven," and the chieftain leader of the locusts. It is interesting to note that in the typical Bedouin romance of Antar we read:

> "The locust is introduced as the national emblem of the Ishmaelites. And it is a remarkable coincidence that Mohammedan tradition speaks of locusts having dropped into the hands of Mohammed, bearing on their wings this inscription—'We are the army of the Great God.' "[24]

Uncommon Valor

Furthermore we read:

> *The locusts looked like horses prepared for battle. On their heads they wore something like crowns of gold, and their faces resembled human faces. Their hair was like women's hair, and their teeth were like lion's teeth. They had breastplates like breastplates of iron, and the sound of their wings was like the thundering of many horses and chariots rushing into battle.*
>
> Revelation 9:7-9

The reference to horses in the symbolism would naturally

lend itself to an interpretation of cavalry. The writer does not say that the riders wore crowns, but had something on their heads that **resembled** crowns. No particular shape is designated by the word *stephanos*, so perhaps the word crown does not quite express the intent here. The true notion of John was to suggest that there was something unusual upon the heads of these warriors, like crowns. Some sort of head dress— like a turban. The turban was uncommon in John's day, but by the time of Jerome (two centuries before the Saracen invasions), Antar wrote a poem about the Arabians:

> "He adjusted himself properly, twisted his whiskers, and folded up his hair under his turban, drawing it from off his shoulders . . . "[25]

It is obvious from Antar's description of these warriors that they do not look like normal warriors. They are uncommon as warriors or not natural in appearance. However, this does not affect their valor or ferocity as warriors, who were well noted for their scorpion-like "sting." These uncommon warriors were told not to hurt the grass or vegetation, which was (and still is) so precious in the Middle eastern desert regions. This agrees exactly with the spirit of the Koran which commands that they should not destroy the palm trees, fruit trees, etc. It is interesting to note that Mohammed himself violated his own laws in his invasion of Tayaf when he ordered the extirpation of the area fruit trees. In modern times it has been common to see a scorched-earth policy, which is uncommon to the Koran, or to the Hebrews. The torching of the oil wells in Kuwait, and the eco-terror policy of Saddam Hussein in the Persian Gulf reveals that he is not a true follower of the Koran! Saddam was merely using religion to try and unite the Arabs under his Hitler-like policies against Israel and the western "infidel" world.

The Battle Of Tours

Mohammed was born in the year A.D. 570. His family was probably one of the priestly families of Mecca, although the family fortunes were at a low ebb at the time of his birth. At an early age he lost his parents and grew up with relatives. He became a camel driver and went on long trips with caravans, going as far as Syria and possibly Egypt. Without a doubt, a great deal that later went into the Koran, the sacred book of Islam, was learned during these years of travel. He married a rich widow, and it was during these times of leisure that he began his visions, and heard the "voices" calling him to be a prophet. His wealthy wife encouraged him, and the rest is history. The initial years were rough as it is hard to convince people that you're a prophet—even Moses found that out. Mohammed's flight from his enemies, now referred to as "The Hegira," occurred in A.D. 622 and marks a turning point in his life and the Islamic faith.

By the time of his death, in A.D. 632, he was master of Arabia, and his banners had been carried as far as Syria. He had even sent letters to the emperors of the Roman and Persian empires asking that they become his followers. They laughed at him, but the next 150 years witnessed amazing growth, as predicted by the writer John (see Revelation 9:5). The armies of Mohammed swarmed like locusts over the Middle eastern world covering territory larger than the Roman emperors had ever dreamed of conquering. The turning point of the world came to a place called Tours, when in A.D. 732 Charles Martel, with a ragtag army miraculously defeated the locust-like Muslims, saving the western world from sure defeat! As I see it, had God not used Charles Martel at the Battle of Tours, Christianity would have been hard pressed to survive. This battle was one of the most important battles in the history of the world, and in fulfillment of the ultimate plans of God. This battle was predicted by God:

> *From the time that the daily sacrifice is abolished and the abomination that causes desolation is set up, there will be 1,290 days. Blessed is the one who waits for and reaches the end of the 1,335 days.*
> Daniel 12:11-12

583 B.C. (Sacrifices abolished) + A.D. 732 (Battle of Tours) = 1,335 Hebrew days or 1,315 solar years.

Or, 1,315 Solar Years – 583 B.C. = A.D. 732 (Battle of Tours)

I hope you can sense the immense importance of this battle which gave a *wound to the beast* (see Revelation 13:14), but did not kill it. John says the beast was *wounded by the sword and yet lived.* Charles Martel stopped the beast but did not kill it. It has resurrected its ghastly head again in these last days and eventually will give us the Anti-christ. So the Anti-christ will come from the Leopard/Bear/Lion empire, and not the Roman empire as is often taught today! Some leader, like Saddam Hussein, will unite the Arab world (Leopard/Bear/Lion), and muster again all his forces (locusts) against Israel.

Unmasking The Beast

Many people have expected the Anti-christ to come from the West, namely, a revived Roman Empire. No where does scripture make that prediction. On the contrary, he will be the Beast of the East, possessing qualities of those empires that have gone before, i.e., the Lion, Bear, and Leopard. Remember, these are qualities of the Babylonian, Medo-Persian, and Grecian empires. A Leopard is noted for its bloodthirstiness and cruelty and swiftness. The idea of Bear-like feet is strength. A bears strength is in its feet and claws.

The Lion, well noted as king of the beasts is vicious in its hold. Once it takes hold of a victim, it does not let go! All together John is saying the eighth beast will have qualities of activity, bloodthirstiness, strength, and ferocity—all symbols of a tyrannical power. Also note the geographical location of these empires surrounding the Persian Gulf area.

The beast I saw resembled a leopard, but had feet like those of a bear, and a mouth like that of a lion . . .
Revelation 13:2

Observe the working backwards from the Grecian Empire to Babylon. The writer has distinctly set forth the fact that the last phase, or final Gentile Empire will be linked with all that has gone before. Thereby incorporating into this last great Confederacy all the chief elements of each of the three eastern civilizations that have left a mark upon the world.

The beast who once was, and now is not, is an eighth king. He belongs to the seven and is going to his destruction.
Revelation 17:11

In other words, he is out of the seven as previously discussed, and will be from the east. He will unite in himself all the God-opposed characteristics of the former three empires (Leopard/Bear/Lion).

Almost In The Obituary Column

One of the heads of the beast seemed to have a fatal wound, but the fatal wound had been healed.
Revelation 13:3

I have endeavored to show throughout this book that the word "beast" is symbolically used to represent an empire. Keep in mind, however, that each beastly empire was led by a beast-like individual, such as: Nebuchadnezzar, Alexander, Hitler, etc. This last beast-led, beastly empire tops them all! History reveals how everything shifted to the western civilization and the new world. The cradle of civilization, along with ancient Babylon, became not a cradle, but a grave for centuries and centuries. Then with the advent of Mohammed there was a sudden resurgence of power until Charles Martel stopped it in A.D. 732. Martel caused a "wound to death" of the advance of the Islamic faith, which incidentally covered the same territory as the Lion, Bear, and Leopard. This was not a coincidence but Providence at work! Only until recent history, especially since World War II, and 1948 (when Israel became a nation again), has attention shifted back to the middle east. Part of the reason has been the discovery of oil. The area is filthy rich with black gold—and the western world is totally dependent upon it. This wicked eighth beast is to ascend, as it were, out of the Abyss. For it is Satanic power that will bring into existence what is depicted here. It will be the devil's last ditch effort to make men believe that they do not need Jesus Christ.

H.A. Ironside has an old work on Revelation that is timeless. It was republished in 1930. With regards to the eighth beast, Ironside says:

> "He will be a man of marvelous appearance and transcendant ability, wholly given up to Satan. He will be the great civil leader of the last days—the man who will have the final word in all matters, religious as well. All the civilized world will wonder after him, do homage to him and his hidden master, the devil. In his pride and folly he will speak great and blasphemous things against God. He will doubtless consider himself the man of destiny whom no power, human or divine, can overthrow . . . this coming one is the Grand Monarch of the New Age cult. He is the coming Mahdi . . . the long expected last incarnation of Vishnu waited for by the Brahmins; the coming Montezuma of the Aztecs; the false Messiah of

79

the Apostate Jews; the great Master of all sects of Yogis; the Ultimate Man of the evolutionists; the *Uebermensch* of Nietzsche . . . he will be Satan controlled, God defying, merciless, almost super human. An individual whose manifestation will mean the consummation of the present apostasy, and the full deification of humanity to his bewildered dupes."[26]

Since this eighth beast is representative of the final great empire to exist on the earth, and led by Anti-christ, it seems appropriate that another beast "two horns like a lamb, and speaking as a dragon" represents the apostate church—or a religious organization that pays homage to the first beast.

Remember back in 1973 when we had to wait in line to buy gasoline? Middle eastern nations had formed an alliance called OPEC, and they dictated to the world the price of gas and oil. It especially affected the western world and in our local communities produced long lines at the pumps. Just as OPEC dictated prices, so will this final apostate organization dictate what you can buy or sell. I suspect that oil again will play a big role in all this. For we are told:

> . . . *no one could buy or sell unless he had the mark . . .*
> Revelation 13:17

Marked For Life

The *mark* referred to is either the name of the beast, or the number of his name. The meaning, whether figurative or literal, is that there will be no question as to one's allegiance to the beast. Just as a Christian is "marked" by the Holy Spirit, or sealed, so will those followers of the beast be "marked" to him, as a slave was marked or stamped to his master. Soldiers punctured their arms with the marks of the general under whom they served. Modern day sailors often tattoo the name of the ship to which they are assigned upon their bodies. Antiochus Epiphanes branded the Jews with the ivy leaf, the pagan symbol of Bacchus. It is well documented that Hitler had his Jewish victims "stamped" or "marked" as they were incarcerated and led to their houses of slaughter. We are told that the beast will cause:

> *. . . everyone, small and great, rich and poor, free and slave, to receive a mark on his right hand or on his forehead.*
> Revelation 13:16

The mark on the right hand and forehead implies prostration of body and intellect to the beast! On the forehead for profession or affirmation; and on the hand for work or service.

In addition we are told that his number is 666. Most people are anxious for some kind of interpretation, as there have been tons of speculation or sensational theories developed as to the mark of the beast, and the number 666. As Barclay pointed out, the ancient world had no figures for numbers, therefore the letters of the alphabet did duty for numbers as well. Thus an A represented 1, B represented 2, etc. Graffiti found on the walls of Pompeii said: "I love her whose number is 545." Thus the anonymous lover wrote and concealed his love in the same sentence! To illustrate how this works an enterprising biblical student worked out the formula for Hitler during World War II. And Hitler, as we have discovered, certainly was a type of Anti-christ. The formula was:

Let A = 100, B = 101, C = 102, etc.

The sum of H-I-T-L-E-R added up to 666. This probably drove fear into a lot of people!

Only recently did I hear further speculation on the number 666. The speaker presented a very interesting point. He claimed that the recent United Nations resolution passed condemning Iraq was 665. And that the next U.N. Resolution would be

666, condemning Israel! Well, I mean to tell you, he had my attention there. But before I got too excited, I decided to double check. I went to the public library and asked for the Resolution condemning Iraq prior to the Gulf War. To my surprise there were 12 U.N. Resolutions! In response to Iraq's invasion of Kuwait the United Nations Security Council passed 12 resolutions from August 2 to November 29, 1990 (Resolutions 660-662; 664-667; 669-670; 674; and 677-678). I quote Resolution 665 exactly as I found it in the public library:

> Resolution 665, Aug. 25, 1990: Called upon U.N. members to join a naval armada to enforce economic sanctions by inspecting and verifying cargoes and destinations of all ships in the Persian Gulf region. (adopted 13-0; Cuba and Yemen abstained).

Resolution 666, which the speaker claimed would be the next one condemning Israel has already been enacted. I quote it here:

> Resolution 666, Sept. 13, 1990: Reiterated Iraq's responsibility for the safety and well-being of foreigners in Iraq and Kuwait and imposed strict limitations on shipments of food and humanitarian aid to Iraq and Kuwait. (Adopted 13-2; Cuba and Yemen voted against).

As anyone can see the United Nations has already enacted Resolution 666, but the speaker led his audience to believe that Resolution 665 dealt solely with the Gulf War, and the world sets waiting for the apocalyptic Resolution 666! What a farce! This is gross misinterpretation of scripture, and a total lack of scholarship, which shouldn't be found in the camp of the Lord. It is sensationalism at its best, or should I say worst! Most people in the audience never thought to check out the veracity and scholarship of the speaker's statement. They took it as the gospel truth! And that is unfortunate.

All I care to say further is, that six is the number for man, and the emphasis in triplicate may be the devil's attempt to emulate God the Father, Son, and Holy Spirit. In other words, Satan, Anti-christ, and unholy spirit (the spirit of anti-christ has long been in the world). Indubitably, when the Anti-christ does appear, and he will when it is time, then the meaning will be clear and so obvious that all who turn to God will be warned to have no fellowship with the unfruitful works of darkness.

U.N. Security Council Resolutions In Response To Iraqi Invasion Of Kuwait

Following are the 12 United Nations Security Council re-solutions passed Aug. 2 to Nov. 29, 1990, in response to Iraq's invasion of Kuwait.

Resolution 660, Aug. 2, 1990:
Condemned the invasion of Kuwait and demanded Iraq's immediate and unconditional withdrawal of troops. Urged both countries to begin peace negotiations. *(Adopted 14-0; Yemen abstained.)*
[See 1990, p. 567E1]

Resolution 661, Aug. 6, 1990:
Imposed a sweeping trade embargo against Iraq and occupied Kuwait and created a special sanctions committee to monitor the embargo. Asked U.N. members to protect Kuwaiti assets worldwide. Called for the restoration of the legitimate Kuwaiti government. *(Adopted 13-0; Cuba and Yemen abstained.)*
[See 1990, p. 581A1]

Resolution 662, Aug. 9, 1990:
Declared the Iraqi annexation of Kuwait "null and void" under international law. *(Adopted unanimously.)*
[See 1990, p. 583E2]

Resolution 664, Aug. 18, 1990:
Demanded the immediate release of, and warned against harming, foreigners in Iraq and Kuwait. Insisted that Iraq repeal its order closing diplomatic and consular missions in Kuwait. *(Adopted unanimously.)*
[See 1990, p. 641B1]

Resolution 665, Aug. 25, 1990:
Called upon U.N. members to join a naval armada to enforce economic sanctions by inspecting and verifying cargoes and destinations of all ships in the Persian Gulf region. *Adopted 13-0; Cuba and Yemen abstained.)*
[See 1990, p. 663A1]

Resolution 666, Sept. 13, 1990:
Reiterated Iraq's responsibility for the safety and well-being of foreigners in Iraq and Kuwait and imposed strict limitations on shipments of food and humanitarian aid to Iraq and Kuwait. *(Adopted 13-2; Cuba and Yemen voted against.)*
[See 1990, p.718D2]

Resolution 667, Sept. 16, 1990:
Condemned Iraq's violation of diplomatic compounds in Kuwait. Demanded the immediate release of foreigners in Iraq and Kuwait. *(Adopted unanimously.)*
[See 1990, p. 685F2]

Resolution 669, Sept. 24, 1990:
Stressed that only the U.N. special sanctions committee was authorized to permit food and other humanitarian aid shipments to Iraq or occupied Kuwait. *(Adopted unanimously.)*
[See 1990, p. 888D2]

THE BEAST OF THE EAST

Resolution 670, Sept. 25, 1990:
Extended the land and sea blockade of Iraq and Kuwait to include an embargo on air traffic, except for authorized humanitarian aid. Called on U.N. members to detain Iraqi ships to prevent them from breaking the naval embargo. *(Adopted 14-1; Cuba against.)*
[See 1990, p. 717A1]

Resolution 674, Oct. 29, 1990:
Detailed Iraqi liability for damages, injuries, and financial losses resulting from the invasion and occupation of Kuwait. Instructed U.N. members to begin preparing claims and collecting data on war crimes. Demanded that Iraq allow the resupply of besieged foreign embassies in Kuwait. *(Adopted 13-0; Cuba and Yemen abstained.)*
[See 1990, p. 805A1]

Resolution 677, Nov. 28, 1990:
Condemned Iraq's destruction of Kuwaiti civil records and its efforts to alter Kuwait's demographic composition. *(Adopted unanimously.)*
[See 1990, p. 888D2]

Resolution 678, Nov. 29, 1990:
Established a Jan. 15, 1991 deadline for Iraq's unconditional surrender and withdrawal from Kuwait. Authorized U.N. members to use force to expel Iraq from Kuwait after the deadline. *(Adopted 12-2; China abstained, and Cuba and Yemen voted against.)*
[See 1990, p. 888E1, text, p. 888A2]

Report 6

THE SANDS OF ARMAGEDDON

T HE Babylonian captivity of seventy years duration was one of the more difficult times for God's covenant people, the Israelites. Israel was literally dead in the water as a nation, deprived of her land, her king, and her beloved temple. Restoration seemed virtually impossible. But God delights in doing the impossible. Enter Ezekiel.

Vision Of The Dry Bones

It was during this difficult period of time that God called forth one of the more colorful prophets—Ezekiel. To stress His sovereign power and that He never reneges on a promise, God gave to Ezekiel the remarkable vision of the Dry Bones.

God transported Ezekiel *by the Spirit* to a Valley of Dry Bones. Ezekiel noticed that the bones had been bleached white in the desert sun. God asked Ezekiel if he thought these bones could come back to life. The prophet hedged his answer by saying *you know Lord.* The Lord then directed Ezekiel to talk to the bones, i.e. prophesy to them. Ezekiel was astonished to see the bones come alive—flesh developed and life entered into these dry skeletal remains.

The vision was given to renew hope. God was telling Ezekiel that all is not what it appears to be. The nation might be at low tide but the fat lady has not sung. The final curtain call is in God's hands, not the Babylonians. The revival of the dry bones signifies Israel's restoration. God said to Ezekiel:

I am going to open your graves and bring you up from them; I will bring you back to the land of Israel.
Ezekiel 37:12

It is because of this latter promise, that I have believed God has not yet fulfilled, in total fruition, this vow.

There has been much debate over this passage. Many Biblical scholars feel it was fulfilled when Israel returned from Babylon. However, the vision seems to imply more. The breath of life that the corpses received symbolized the Holy Spirit. God seems to be talking not only of a physical return to the land, but also a spiritual rebirth. Many today claim that the return to the land in 1948 fulfilled this promise. Perhaps they are right. At least it was a beginning of fulfillment, but surely we cannot say that Israel has returned to the land filled with the Holy Spirit. No one would deny that Israel has a national spirit, especially when they say: "No more Masada!" Or, we will "never again give up our land." And with the present disintegration of the Soviet Union, many Jews formerly held behind the iron curtain are now allowed to return to their homeland. However, because of the enormity of this passage I cannot believe that we have seen the ultimate fulfillment of the prophecy . . . but perhaps the beginning. There seems to be some catalyst, yet to occur, that will cause Israel to forsake other Gentile nations, even the comfort of the United States, to return to her land.

THE SANDS OF ARMAGEDDON

Two Sticks

Ezekiel's second sign in this vision has to do with confirmation, or explanation of the first. Ezekiel was told to take two sticks of wood and bring them together as one. The two sticks symbolize Judah and Ephraim.

Some have labored to claim that the two sticks represent the Bible (Judah) and the Book of Mormon (Ephraim). However this theory is a wild attempt to satisfy those (Mormons) who want credibility for the Book of Mormon. Others have presented a more interesting proposition that the stick of Ephraim represents the United States of America. After all, we are Israel's lone ally in the world. Proponents of this theory claim that the ten lost tribes, represented by Ephraim, are really the United States, and finally God brings them together as one nation. I have read some powerful arguments along this line of thinking but still it lacks full scriptural support. The great mystery of the Bible, of course, is the United States. Is the U.S. mentioned in scripture? Dr. Charles R. Taylor in his little book: *The Destiny of America*, attempts to answer "yes" to the question by using Isaiah 18 for support. E.H. Skolfield in his book *Hidden Beast 2* has what I call the "Speak softly but carry a big stick" theory. He claims Ephraim is hidden within the U.S. until the appropriate time. At God's time this stick will be brought together with Judah in the holy land. Meanwhile, this is why the U.S. is the lone ally of Israel! Both Taylor and Skolfield have some very interesting theories that are tempting to dig into, but I'm going to resist it. I'm afraid the theories are more sensational than expositional, so I'll decline.

The Two Become One

Regardless of all the above discussion, the two sticks ultimately represent the people of Israel coming together as a single nation. And David will be their King! I do not think this is David resurrected, as some would lead us to believe, but the One of the lineage of David—the Son of God. He is the true Shepherd. It is obvious that none of this has been fulfilled as Israel remains a people scattered all over the world, and the Messiah has not returned. In the U.S. alone there are approximately six million Jews, more than in all of Israel (around four million). There are 700,000 Jews in France (400,000 in Paris which are equal to the 400,000 in Jerusalem). There are over 300,000 Jews in England, etc. According to my 1988 Almanac there were nearly 18 million Jews in the world, so a lot of Jews have to return in great numbers to fulfill this prophecy.

The prophecy does not say that all the Jews will be saved. Some people act as if 100% of the Jews will be saved when He comes because they will *look on Him whom they have pierced (John 20:37)*. It is obvious that they (the Jews) will see Him when He comes, as well as the rest of the world, but where do we read that **all the world** will be saved, or **all** the Jews? If that be the case, then salvation is a "gimme"— as I say when my golf ball is three inches from the hole! Any student of the Bible knows that is not the case, neither the intent of this passage, nor the doctrine of the Bible.

The Gog Factor

Israel has long been tramped on. She is not willing to continue as the world's doormat. In Ezekiel 38 and 39 we are told about Gog and Magog. Volumes have been written about this famous invasion of Israel. Gog is to be the leader of many nations referred to as Magog. Most writers seem to be of general consensus on that point—that Gog is the leader. The task is to determine who is Gog and where is Magog? Again, most agree that "Gog" is a symbolic name for leader of chieftain of a Confederation of Nations that decide to invade Israel.

The words "land of Magog" indicate the land area over which Gog rules, or at least, has tremendous influence. The term "Magog" probably refers to the area north of the Caucasus Mountains. A look at the map will identify the area as part of the Soviet Union, or Russia. Apparently Gog will lead this federation of nations against Israel. The nations are named by the writer and include: Iran (Persia), northern Ethiopia (Cush), Libya (Put), and Turkey (Meshech). That this is not an exhaustive list is shown in Exekiel 38:6: *And many people with thee.* This prophecy anticipates an extensive and massive alliance of powers along with Russia against tiny Israel.

Gog and his allies will advance like a storm and a cloud (Ezekiel 38:16) against Israel who appears to be dwelling in relative safety. Apparently peace was worked out with the Palestinians and the Arabs sometime after the dust settled from the Persian Gulf War. I would foresee this happening in the 90's. Presently Secretary Baker is finding frustration at resolving the Israeli-Palestinian problem even as I write these words. The one to emerge suddenly on the scene to resolve these problems, no doubt, will be the beast of the east. He'll be "Man of the Year" on *Time* magazine, and will probably receive the Nobel Peace prize as a result.

Gog's purpose of attack will come from all sides against Israel. Gog will come from the far north, Iran from the east, Ethiopia and Libya from the south. This awesome army will overrun all obstacles as effortlessly as a cloud sailing across the sky.[27]

The order of the attack is documented in Ezekiel 38:15-21. For correlation Daniel gives us the precise time and manner of the attack:

> *At the time of the end the king of the South will engage him in battle, and the king of the North will storm out against him with chariots and cavalry and a great fleet of ships . . .*
>
> Daniel 11:40

In my reading I learned that four major thoughts are presented by Daniel regarding this war:

(1) The initial action of the war takes place at the time of the end, or in the last days.

(2) The attack is against "him"—the Beast of the East, although directed against Israel.

(3) The attack begins from the south.

(4) The Russians (Gog and her Magog forces) join in *like a whirlwind* or storm from the north.

Two major problems are presented by this "end time" war which I have never seen discussed:

(1) Why would Satan stir up the nations against his own henchman, the Beast?

(2) Where is the U.S. in all this if she is Israel's number one ally?

The Kingdom of darkness stands in sharp contrast to the Kingdom of Light. Even Satan is not divided against himself, as his goal is to destroy the church, and the Jew in order to discredit Jesus Christ. I think Satan realizes he cannot displace God so he attempts to be equal with God. I sometimes

92

wonder that if Satan wants a piece of the action why doesn't he just go off into a far corner of the universe and create his own little world? It's because he can't. Although purely conjecture, I think his best effort at creating was in making a mosquito—a miserable pesty little disease-bearing blood sucker! So, he roams the earth in an attempt to upset the apple cart. But why does he allow rebellion against his "anointed" henchman, the Beast of the East?

Again, this is purely conjecture, as no one knows for sure. Just as it is conjecture as why Judas wanted to betray his Lord. Obviously, Satan is always promoting war, as war brings death, famine, disease, etc. Since Satan was the one who instigated the alleged peace via his beastly diplomat, it would be nothing for him to break it. After all, he is a liar! And master deceptionist. Thus he stirs up Gog and Magog, and the nations thereof, in a last ditch effort to virtually destroy Israel who has been lulled into thinking peace. It just may be that the Beast of the East will use covert diplomacy to prod the nations of Magog into attacking Israel. He baits them at a time when Israel is totally off guard. If they win, Israel is destroyed, and if they lose, they're out of the way creating a vacuum of power into which the Beast can step. Either way he wins!

The "911" Nation

But where is the United States? One of the characteristics of this beast will be diplomacy. He will, no doubt, be a political cat. In obtaining peace for the middle east he undoubtedly lays the ground work by speaking before Congress and the U.N. I suspect that he will seek total support from Congress, which they will be more than glad to give. You recall that President Bush did the smart thing prior to launching Desert Storm by having the U.N. and the Congress endorse sanctions, and/or use force. As a result, his popularity soared to 92% directly following the war. The Beast will do the same thing, after all, the world is weary of the Israeli-Palestinian problem. Here's a man who can fix it! I suspect that the Beast will seek to bind the U.S. to some type of agreement whereby they don't interfere in any shape or form. Congress will be more than happy to go along with such a proposal, as the U.S. cannot continue to be "911" for the world. We have enough domestic problems of our own, and our national debt continues to soar upward.

Another possibility is that the U.S. may have become part of a new "world order" out of the post Gulf-War era. Desert Storm has settled and peace is finally obtained via the help of this dynamic new leader who has burst upon the scene like a prophet. He is from the Leopard/Bear/Lion continuum and understands the problems of the Middle East! After achieving the impossible this man can do no wrong, at least for the time being. His picture is ubiquitous and his name has become a household word. The world applauds the Beast of the East, not knowing it stands at the eleventh hour . . . the sands of Armageddon are blowing.

Gog's Ruin

The campaign of Gog and Magog is a pre-determined disaster from the start. Ezekiel promises that it will end in utter ruin for Gog and her forces. It will be even more disastrous than Iraq's effort against the Desert Storm Coalition Forces. Ezekiel predicts:

I am against you, O Gog, chief prince of Meshech and Tubal. I will turn you around and drag you along . . . On the mountains of Israel you will fall, you and all your troops and the nations with you . . . you will fall in the

open field, for I have spoken, declares the Sovereign Lord.
Ezekiel 39:1-5

Gog's ruin is God's catalyst. As the land of Israel shall be the scene of Gog's wicked attack so shall it be the scene of God's awful punishment inflicted upon Gog. Gog becomes Ezekiel's typical symbol of Satan's designs to destroy the covenant children. Each time he has attempted, he has ended in failure. This campaign is no different in that it sets darkness against light. The measure, speed, and proportion of Gog's defeat is such that Jews all over the world finally realize that they need to go home. The world does not offer sanctuary. Safety and security is only found in God. The sands of Armageddon are now flowing freely through the hourglass. Time is short. Jews from the four corners of the earth are booking passage on El-Al to Tel Aviv.

Armageddon Has Arrived

Gog is out of the way. The Beast of the East is now free to do as he pleases. No longer Mr. Nice Guy. His true colors begin to show. Instead of a friend of Israel he is their worst enemy. And he has a cohort in crime.

Then I saw another beast, coming out of the earth. He had two horns like a lamb, but he spoke like a dragon . . .
Revelation 13:11

This beast has power like the first beast, and he causes all men to worship the first beast. Elsewhere he is called the *False prophet* (Revelation 16:13; 19:20; 20:10). This second beast has two horns like a lamb. But he is counterfeit—a false prophet. Some have speculated that this second beast is the Anti-christ, (Augustine felt so). He performs miracles, signs, wonders, etc. He causes those who worship the first beast to have a *mark* of identification. I've already discussed this mark business, and it may or may not be literal. It appears that the second beast is a pointer, or pseudo John the Baptist, if you will, for the first beast. Now do you see how Satan seeks to duplicate God?

For those Christians who refuse to worship the Beast or to be identified with him—they will be sorely tested, persecuted, and killed. Lines will be drawn like in the days of Rome. Either you declare Caesar as Lord or the Lord as Lord! Choices will have to be made. But even though many will be killed, they will still get the victory over the Beast (Revelation 15:2). To reject the Beast, and to maintain a witness for Christ, even in death, is how God's people overcome both Satan and his Beast. I am reminded of the words of Shadrach, Meshach, and Abednego as they faced the prospects of a fiery death:

> *O Nebuchadnezzar, we do not need to defend ourselves before you in this matter. If we are thrown into the blazing furnace, the God we serve is able to save us from it, and he will rescue us from your hand, O king. But even if he does not, we want you to know, O king, that we will not serve your gods or worship the image of gold you have set up.*
>
> Daniel 3:16-18

These will be perilous times for Israel and Christians. Many who are weak in the faith will fall away. The pressures will separate the wheat from the tares. Paul writes prophetically of this time:

> *Don't let anyone deceive you . . . that day will not come until the rebellion occurs and the man of lawlessness is revealed . . .*
>
> II Thessalonians 2:3

THE SANDS OF ARMAGEDDON

In these last hours this lawless Beast will be busy securing support in his all out effort to rid the world of Christians and Jews. Unfortunately he will not be alone, as he finds willing helpers, even as Hitler did during World War II. The western world, descendants of the Roman Empire, now racked by moral decay of the centuries, will side with the Eighth Beast, for *one hour* (see Revelation 17:12-14), or, for a short period of time. These western leaders known to vacillate back and forth, will go with the flow, and give *power and strength* to the Beast. The world will undoubtedly accept the beastly portrayal that the Judeo-Christian ethic is the root cause of all problems and should be eliminated. Lines will be drawn for this final great conflict—Armageddon has arrived.

Report 7

THE WHITE HORSE RIDER

I T is the old, old story all over again. The underdog versus the odds-on favorite. It's Moses versus Pharaoh. David against Goliath. Elijah against the 400 false prophets of Baalim. No longer is it Jew and Gentile—now it's light versus darkness, and the Vegas odds are on darkness. The entire history of mankind has come down to Armageddon.

> *Then they gathered the kings together to the place that in Hebrew is called Armageddon.*   Revelation 16:16

The word, Armageddon, is compounded from the Hebrew *har megiddon,* or "hill of Megiddo." Megiddo was excavated between 1926-1936 by the Oriental Institute of the University of Chicago. Excavations covering an area of 13 acres revealed the remains of 20 superimposed cities, each city represented by a distinct layer of ruins. Among the very important discoveries are Solomon's stables which were capable of housing 450 horses and 150 chariots, grain silos, etc. Solomon saw Megiddo as a very important defense center located on the southern edge of the plain of Jezreel where the battle of Armageddon is to be fought. The valley itself has a triangular shape of 15 × 15 × 20 miles. It was famous in ancient times for its fertility, and is still known today as the "bread basket of Israel." Many famous battles have been fought in this great valley, and Napoleon Bonaparte upon viewing the valley from the hill of Megiddo exclaimed: "all the armies in the world could fight here." Napoleon wasn't far from the truth!

Silver Bullets

At long last the great moment has arrived.

After this I heard what sounded like the roar of a great multitude in heaven shouting: Hallelujah! Salvation and glory and power belong to our God . . . For the wedding of the Lamb has come . . . I saw heaven standing open and there before me was a white horse, whose rider is called Faithful and True. With justice he judges and makes war.
Revelation 19:1-11

Just in the nick of time, the Great Rider upon the white horse appears to save His people. There is not a better ending. I remember as a kid growing up how I was fascinated by another rider on a white horse, the Lone Ranger. He always seemed to come in the nick of time to save the damsel in distress. And the story always ended with someone asking, "Who was that masked man?" Suddenly you would hear him riding off into the sunset yelling to his white horse: "Hi-yo Silver, away!" Then they would find his silver bullet and exclaim—"The Lone Ranger." Chills went up my spine.

That was story book. This is for real. Silver in the Bible symbolizes redemption. Our salvation rests in and upon the Rider of the White Horse of Revelation 19. When He comes,

He will not leave silver bullets, as his blood has provided us our redemption, neither will He ride off into the future anymore. He did that once, two thousand years ago. Then the angels said to those wondering:

> *Men of Galilee . . . why do you stand here looking into the sky? This same Jesus, who has been taken from you into heaven, will come back in the same way you have seen him go into heaven.*
>
> Acts 1:11

This time He comes for good.

> *For the Lord Himself will come down from heaven, with a loud command, with the voice of the archangel and with the trumpet call of God . . .*
>
> I Thessalonians 4:16

We know this white horse Rider is the Lord Jesus Christ because John tells us:

> *His eyes are like blazing fire, and on his head are many crowns. He has a name written on him that no one knows but he himself. He is dressed in a robe dipped in blood, and his name is the Word of God. The armies of heaven were following him, riding on white horses and dressed in fine linen, white and clean. Out of his mouth comes a sharp sword with which to strike down the nations. He will rule them with an iron scepter. He treads the winepress of the fury of the wrath of God Almighty. On his robe and on his thigh he has this name written: **King of Kings and Lord of Lords.***
>
> Revelation 19:12-16

Lockup

> *Then I saw the beast and the kings of the earth and their armies gathered together to make war against the rider on the horse and his army.*
>
> Revelation 19:19

But this will be the shortest war in the history of mankind. The 100 hour ground assault with Iraq is nothing compared to this war. There is no contest.

... the beast was captured, and with him the false prophet who had performed the miraculous signs on his behalf... The two of them were thrown alive into the fiery lake of burning sulfur.
Revelation 19:20

These armies come from:

... the four corners of the earth—Gog and Magog— to gather them for battle. In number they are like the sand on the seashore.
Revelation 20:8

Gog and Magog here represent the nations of the world and is in contrast to the passage in Ezekiel, as this battle is Armageddon. This gathering is the same as Revelation 16:14 where it speaks of:

... spirits of demons performing miraculous signs, and they go out to the kings of the whole world, to gather them for the battle on the great day of God Almighty.

Satan will never again be allowed to deceive the nations. The first time, due to the sacrifice of Christ, he was *bound for a thousand years,* or a period of time. Then he was set free for a *short time* (Revelation 20:1-3). This time Satan is locked up for good—for eternity.

And the devil, who deceived them, was thrown into the lake of burning sulfur, where the beast and the false prophet had been thrown. They will be tormented day and night for ever and ever.
Revelation 20:10

Payday

The fascinating thing about Revelation 20 is what people have made it say. This passage says nothing about a literal throne of David or a restored Jewish Kingdom on earth. It says nothing about a rebuilt Jewish temple. And certainly does not teach the renewal of animal sacrifices, which would be an abominable addendum to the Sacrifice of Christ on the cross! In the book of Hebrews we read:

> . . . *so Christ was sacrificed once to take away the sins of many people; and he will appear a second time, not to bear sin, but to bring salvation to those who are waiting for him.*
>
> Hebrews 9:28

When Christ returns it is payback time. All those who have cried:

> *How long, Sovereign Lord, holy and true, until you judge the inhabitants of the earth and avenge our blood?*
>
> Revelation 6:10

They will have to wait no longer. It may seem like an eternity for those who go through tribulation awaiting justice. But remember, the Hebrew children prayed for over 400 years for a deliverer to take them out of Egypt. Peter wrote:

> . . . *do not forget this one thing . . . With the Lord a day is like a thousand years, and a thousand years are like a day. The Lord is not slow in keeping his promise . . . But the day of the Lord will come like a thief. The heavens will disappear with a roar; the elements will be destroyed by fire, and the earth and everything in it will be laid bare.*
>
> II Peter 3:8-10

103

No Waiting In Line

When Christ returns there will be no more waiting. You will not be asked to take a number and wait. Don't ask me how Christ will do it. All I know is He will do it. It will be all wrapped up immediately.

> *Then I saw a great white throne and him who was seated on it. Earth and sky fled from his presence, and there was no place for them. And I saw the dead, great and small, standing before the throne, and books were opened. Another book was opened, which was the book of life. The dead were judged according to what they had done as recorded in the books . . . If anyone's name was not found written in the book of life, he was thrown into the lake of fire.*
> Revelation 20:11-15

Genesis II

The final two chapters of the Revelation describe God's plan to begin anew . . .

> *I saw a new heaven and a new earth, for the first heaven and the first earth had passed away, and there was no longer any sea.*
> Revelation 21:1

I call this Genesis II, and it follows the deluge of fire. The first deluge was water (Genesis 6 & 7), which only Noah and his immediate family survived. This deluge is by fire, for even the earth must be cleansed in preparation. Peter said:

> *. . . the day of the Lord will come like a thief. The heavens will disappear with a roar; the elements will be destroyed by fire, and the earth and everything in it will be laid bare.*
> II Peter 3:10

John claims there will be no more sea. What he is probably saying is there will be no more turmoil. The word "sea" often depicts (symbolically) the nations. As you recall, the final beast is from the sea of nations—more specifically the Leopard/Lion/Bear region of the nations. And it was the nations gathered like a sea in the Valley of Jezreel to do battle.

Genesis II will be superior to Genesis I, for now rebellion is put down forever. And forever is a long time! You recall in Genesis I there was a beautiful garden (paradise). But there was also Satan's presence and the possibility of temptation to sin due to choice. In Genesis II Satan will not be present as he has been forever cast into the lake of fire with the beast and false prophet. Thus sin, or the possibility of sin has been eliminated forever! Choices are made prior to Genesis II.

If anyone's name was not found written in the book of life, he was thrown into the lake of fire.
Revelation 20:15

In Genesis II there will be no more:

- **Sin**—Darkness is gone forever and there is no need for the sun or moon as Light comes from the Lamb of God!

- **Death** (or pain or crying)—The last enemy to be conquered is death which is the curse due to sin.

    . . . Death has been swallowed up in victory. Where, O death, is your victory? Where, O death, is your sting? The sting of death is sin, and the power of sin is the law. But thanks be to God! He gives us the victory through our Lord Jesus Christ.
    I Corinthians 15:54-57

- **Unbelievers**—This eliminates the turmoil and offers peace and security for we discover that on no day will the gates of the new city ever be shut!

105

Dispensations of:

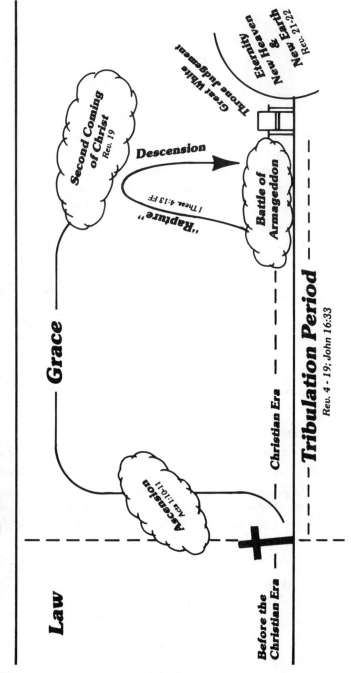

Law

Grace

Before the Christian Era

Ascension
Acts 1:10-11

Second Coming of Christ
Rev. 19

Descension

"Rapture"
I Thess. 4:13 FF

Battle of Armageddon

Great White Throne Judgement

Eternity
New Heaven & New Earth
Rev. 21-22

— + — Christian Era — — —

— — **Tribulation Period** — —

Rev. 4 - 19; John 16:33

Epilogue

The arguement is often pressed that if Anti-christ is to come, first will we not be looking for the Anti-christ rather than Christ? In reading the New Testament I discover that Jesus predicted the fall of Jerusalem before His return. Paul knew this when he wrote II Thessalonians around A.D. 54. Jerusalem did not fall until A.D. 70. Was Paul urging the Thessalonians to look for the Roman soldiers? No way, for he said:

> . . . *the day of the Lord will come like a thief in the night . . .*
>
> I Thessalonians 5:2

And he wrote:

> . . . *for that day will not come, until the rebellion occurs and the man of lawlessness is revealed, the man doomed to destruction.*
>
> II Thessalonians 2:3

Christians can surely note the signs that His coming is imminent. Knowing about these signs should not take the edge off the urgency of His coming. In fact, it should sharpen the edge!

During the first year of our marriage my wife discovered some tracks outside our bedroom window. There had been talk in our town of a rambling voyeur—or peeping Tom. In order to prove to my wife that I was one of the last remaining cavaliers, I hid myself in the bushes to catch this beast. But he never showed again, and after several uneventful nights, I grew tired of the ordeal and quit watching for him. Had I seen more signs I would have continued my stake-out with enthusiasm! Paul, and Jesus too, urged us to watch for the signs. The signs are so evident today that we should be more diligent than ever in our watchfullness! Since 1967 Gentile domination has ended in Jerusalem. The Jews now control the ancient city of David. This, I believe is crucial, and a major sign. Events are unfolding before our very eyes, which lead us to believe that His coming is soon. Let us not, however, fall into the trap of setting dates as some are given to doing. Even Jesus said:

No one knows about that day or hour, not even the angels in heaven, nor the Son, but only the Father.
                                                    Matthew 24:36

Instead, we should prepare ourselves by making sure we are ready for that Glorious day. Do you believe that Jesus died for your sins, arose from the grave, and is coming again? Can you affirm John 3:16 in your heart? To those who can, there is a special thrill and blessing in reading the Book of Revelation. For the theme of that book is "Jesus is Coming." When I read the final two chapters of John's attempt to describe the future destiny of the believer, I'm reminded of an anecdote of Marco Polo, the famous Venetian traveler of the thirteenth century. As he lay dying, he was urged by his attendants to recant—to withdraw the stories he had told about China and the far east. But he said: "I have not told half of what I saw." Neither could John tell half, or even a hundredth part of what he saw. It was humanly impossible. For how can anyone describe the Glory that awaits the believer in Christ Jesus?

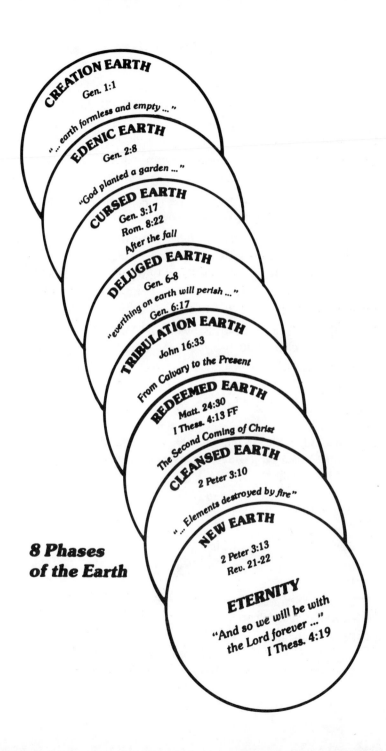

CREATION EARTH
Gen. 1:1
"... earth formless and empty ..."

EDENIC EARTH
Gen. 2:8
"God planted a garden ..."

CURSED EARTH
Gen. 3:17
Rom. 8:22
After the fall

DELUGED EARTH
Gen. 6-8
"everthing on earth will perish ..."
Gen. 6:17

TRIBULATION EARTH
John 16:33
From Calvary to the Present

REDEEMED EARTH
Matt. 24:30
I Thess. 4:13 FF
The Second Coming of Christ

CLEANSED EARTH
2 Peter 3:10
"... Elements destroyed by fire"

NEW EARTH
2 Peter 3:13
Rev. 21-22

ETERNITY
"And so we will be with
the Lord forever ..."
I Thess. 4:19

**8 Phases
of the Earth**

Bibliography

1. Dickey, Christopher, "Sanctuary Underground: The Hussein Hilton," *Newsweek*, February 4, 1991, pp. 40-41.

2. Tenny, Merrill C., *Pictoral Bible Dictionary*, Grand Rapids: Zondervan Publishing House, 1963.

3. Dyer, Charles H., *The Rise Of Babylon*, Wheaton: Tyndale House Publishers, Inc., 1991.

4. Ibid.

5. McKeever, James, "Iraq, Babylon and Oil," *End-Times News Digest*, October, 1990, p. 2.

6. Ibid., p. 3.

7. Barry, John and Evan Thomas, "A Textbook Victory," *Newsweek*, March 11, 1991, p. 42.

8. Ibid.

9. Walvoord, John F., and John E. Walvoord, *Armageddon, Oil, and the Middle East*, Grand Rapids: Zondervan Publishing House, 1980.

10. Leupold, H.C., *Exposition of Genesis*, Grand Rapids: Baker Book House, 1965.

11. Ferguson, John, *Great Events of Bible Times*, Garden City, NY: Doubleday & Company, Inc.

12. Roth, Cecil, *A History of the Jews*, New York: Shocken Books, 1966.

13. Sachar, Abram Leon, *A History of the Jews*, New York: Alfred A. Knopf, Inc., 1965.

14. Ben-David, Shemaya, *Megiddo/Armageddon*, Israel: 1979.

15. McClain, Alva J., *Daniel's Prophecy of the Seventy Weeks*, Grand Rapids: Zondervan Publishing House, 1969.

BIBLIOGRAPHY

16. Roth, 1961.

17. Shipler, David K., *Arab and Jew*, New York: Times Books, 1986.

18. Skolfield, E.H., *Hidden Beast 2*, Fort Myers: Fish House, 1990.

19. Shipler, 1986.

20. Bray, John, *Israel In Bible Prophecy*, Lakeland: John Bray Ministries, 1989.

21. Skolfield, 1990.

22. Roth, 1966.

23. Barclay, William, *The Revelation of John Vol. 2*, Philadelphia: The Westminister Press, 1960.

24. Barnes, Albert, *Notes on the New Testament*, Grand Rapids: Baker Book House, 1965.

25. Ibid., p. 220.

26. Ironside, H.A., *Lectures on the Revelation*, New York: L.B. Printing Company, 1930.

27. Walvoord, John F. and Roy B. Zuck, *The Bible Knowledge Commentary*, Wheaton: Victor Books, 1985.

Books by Starburst Publishers
(Partial listing—full list available on request)

The Beast Of The East
—Alvin M. Shifflett

Asks the questions: Has the Church become involved in a 'late date' comfort mode—expecting to be 'raptured' before the Scuds fall? Should we prepare for a lonmg and arduous Desert Storm to Armageddon battle? Are we ignoring John 16:33, *"In this world you will have trouble?"* (NIV)

(trade paper) ISBN 0914984411 **$6.95**

TemperaMysticism—*Exploding the Temperament Theory*
—Shirley Ann Miller

Former Astrologer reveals how Christians (including some well-respected leaders) are being lured into the occult by practicing the Temperaments (Sanguine, Choleric, Phlegmatic, and Melancholy) and other New Age personality typologies.

(trade paper) ISBN 0914984306 **$8.95**

Except For A Staff
—Randy R. Spencer

Parallels the various functions of the Old Testament shepherd's staff with the ever-present ministry of the Holy Spirit. It sheds new light on the role of the Holy Spirit in the life of the Christian. "You will be blessed and challenged through reading *Except For A Staff,"* Rev. Jerry Falwell.

(trade paper) ISBN 0914984349 **$7.95**

The Quest For Truth
—Ken Johnson

A book designed to lead the reader to a realization that there is no solution to the world's problems, nor is there a purpose to life, apart from Jesus Christ. It is the story of a young man on a symbolic journey in search of happiness and the meaning of life.

(trade paper) ISBN 0914984217 **$7.95**

Like A Bulging Wall
—Robert Borrud

Will you survive the 1990's economic crash? This book shows how debt, greed, and covetousness, along with a lifestyle beyond our means, has brought about an explosive situation in this country. Gives "call" from God to prepare for judgement in America, Also lists TOP-RATED U.S. BANKS and SAVINGS & LOANS.

(trade paper) ISBN 0914984284 **$8.95**

Reverse The Curse In Your Life
—Joan Hake Robie

A handy "guidebook" for those who wish to avoid Satan's snares. Includes Biblical Curses, Forbidden Practices, Warfare Prayers, and much more. This book is the result of author Joan Hake Robie's over ten years of research on the subject of the occult, demons, and Satanism.

(trade paper) ISBN 0914984241 **$7.95**

Purchasing Information: Most listed books are available from your favorite Bookstore, either from current stock or special order . You may also order direct from STARBURST PUBLISHERS. When ordering enclose full payment plus $2.00 for shipping and handling ($2.50 if Canada or Overseas). Payment in US Funds only. Please allow three weeks for delivery. Make checks payable to and mail to STARBURST PUBLISHERS, P.O. Box 4123, LANCASTER, PA 17604. Prices subject to change without notice.   05-92